A Biography
of Malcolm X

by Jessica Gunderson
illustrated by Seitu Hayden

Consultant:
Keith Mayes, PhD
Professor of History and
African American and African Studies
University of Minnesota, Minneapolis

CAPSTONE PRESS
a capstone imprint

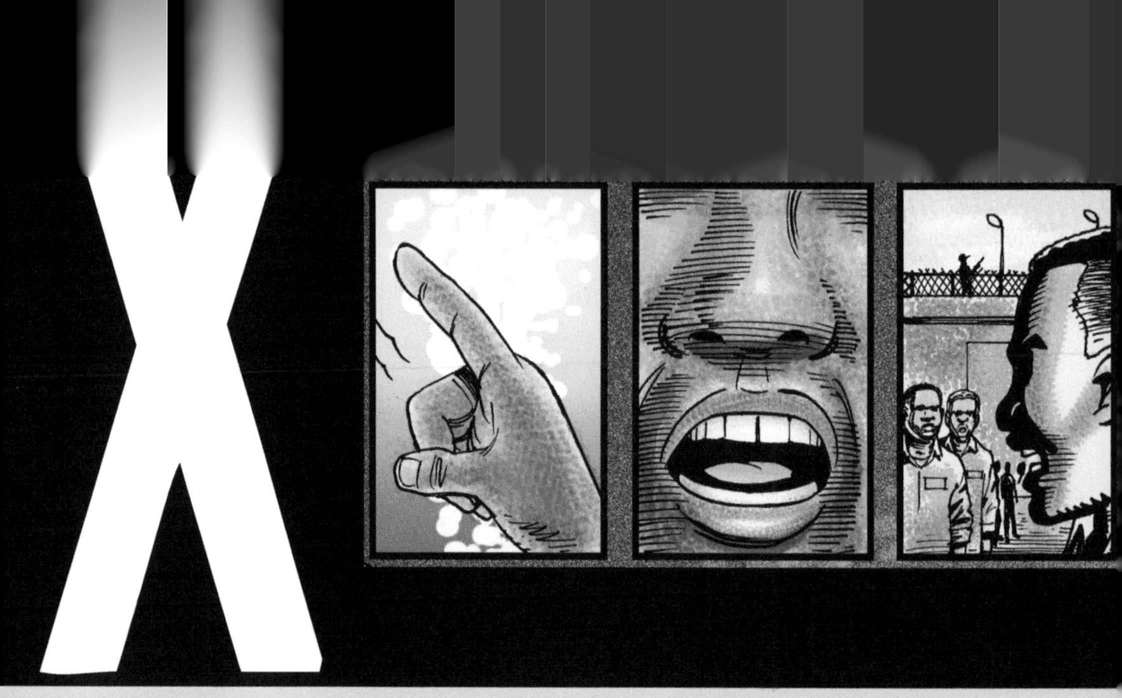

Graphic Library is published by Capstone Press,
1710 Roe Crest Drive
North Mankato, Minnesota 56003.

www.capstonepub.com

Library of Congress Cataloging-in-Publication Data
Gunderson, Jessica.
X : the biography of Malcolm X / by Jessica Gunderson ; illustrated by Seitu Hayden.
p. cm.—(Graphic Library. American graphic)
Summary: "In graphic novel format, explores the life and death of Malcolm X"—Provided by publisher.
Includes bibliographical references and index.
ISBN 978-1-4296-5471-5 (library binding)
ISBN 978-1-4296-6267-3 (paperback)
1. X, Malcolm, 1925-1965—Juvenile literature. 2. African American Muslims—Biography—Juvenile literature. I. Hayden, Seitu. II. Title.
BP223.Z8G86 2011
297.8'7092—dc22
[B] 2010037029

Direct quotations appear in yellow on the following pages:

Pages 12-13, 22 (second and third panels), and 29, from *By Any Means Necessary: Speeches, Interviews, and a Letter by Malcolm X,* George Breitman, ed. (New York: Pathfinder Press, 1970)

Page 17, from *Malcolm X Speaks: Selected Speeches and Statements,* George Breitman, ed. (New York: Merit Publishers, 1965)

Pages 20, 21, 24, and 27, from The *Autobiography of Malcolm X* by Malcolm X and Alex Haley (New York: Grove Press, 1966)

Page 22 (first panel), from *The Last Year of Malcolm X: The Evolution of a Revolutionary,* George Breitman, ed. (New York: Merit Publishers, 1967)

Art Director: Nathan Gassman

Editor: Lori Shores

Media Researcher: Wanda Winch

Production Specialist: Eric Manske

Photo Credits:
Library of Congress, Prints and Photographs Division, 28

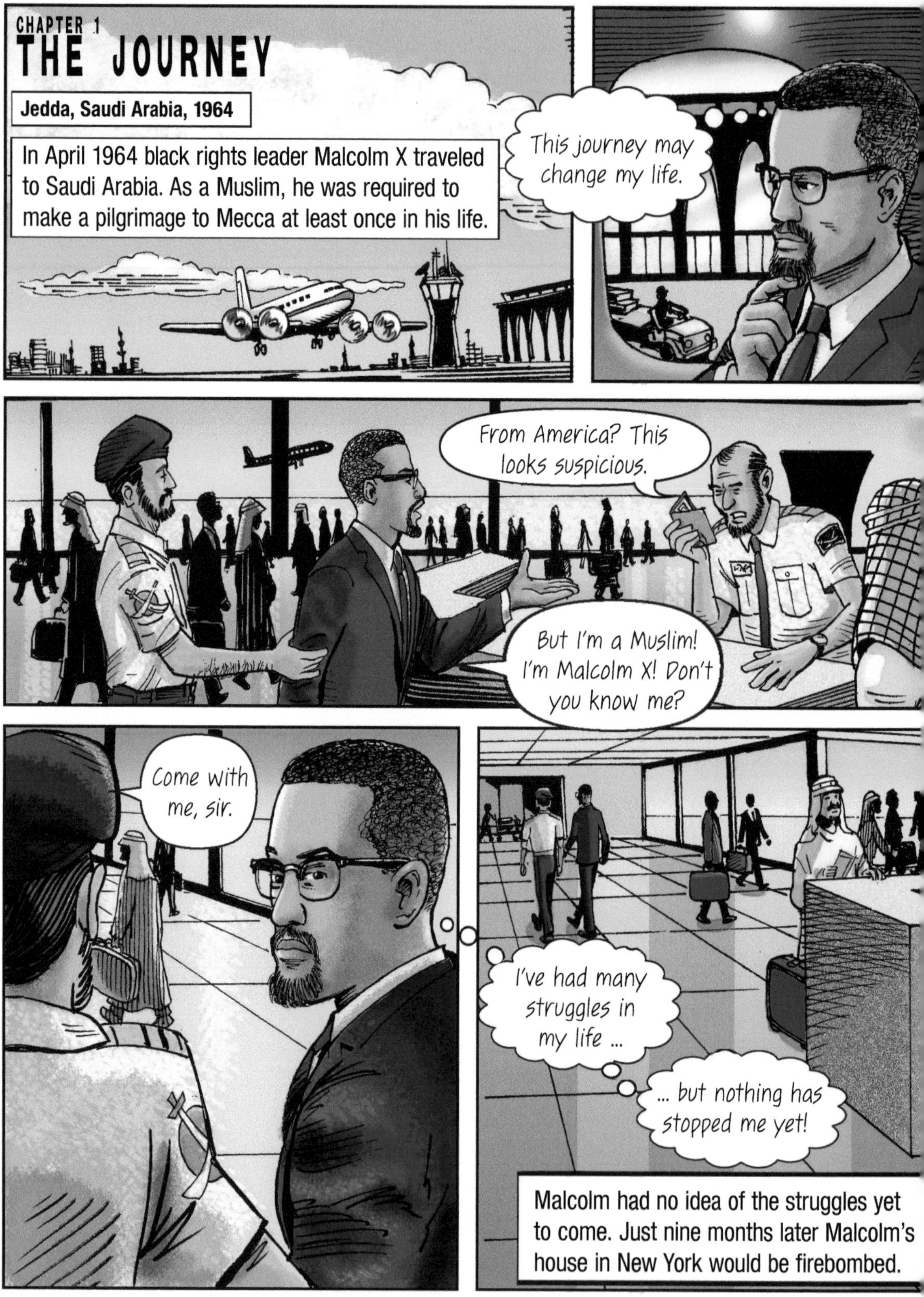
CHAPTER 1
THE JOURNEY
Jedda, Saudi Arabia, 1964
In April 1964 black rights leader Malcolm X traveled to Saudi Arabia. As a Muslim, he was required to make a pilgrimage to Mecca at least once in his life.
This journey may change my life.
From America? This looks suspicious.
But I'm a Muslim! I'm Malcolm X! Don't you know me?
Come with me, sir.
I've had many struggles in my life ...
... but nothing has stopped me yet!
Malcolm had no idea of the struggles yet to come. Just nine months later Malcolm's house in New York would be firebombed.

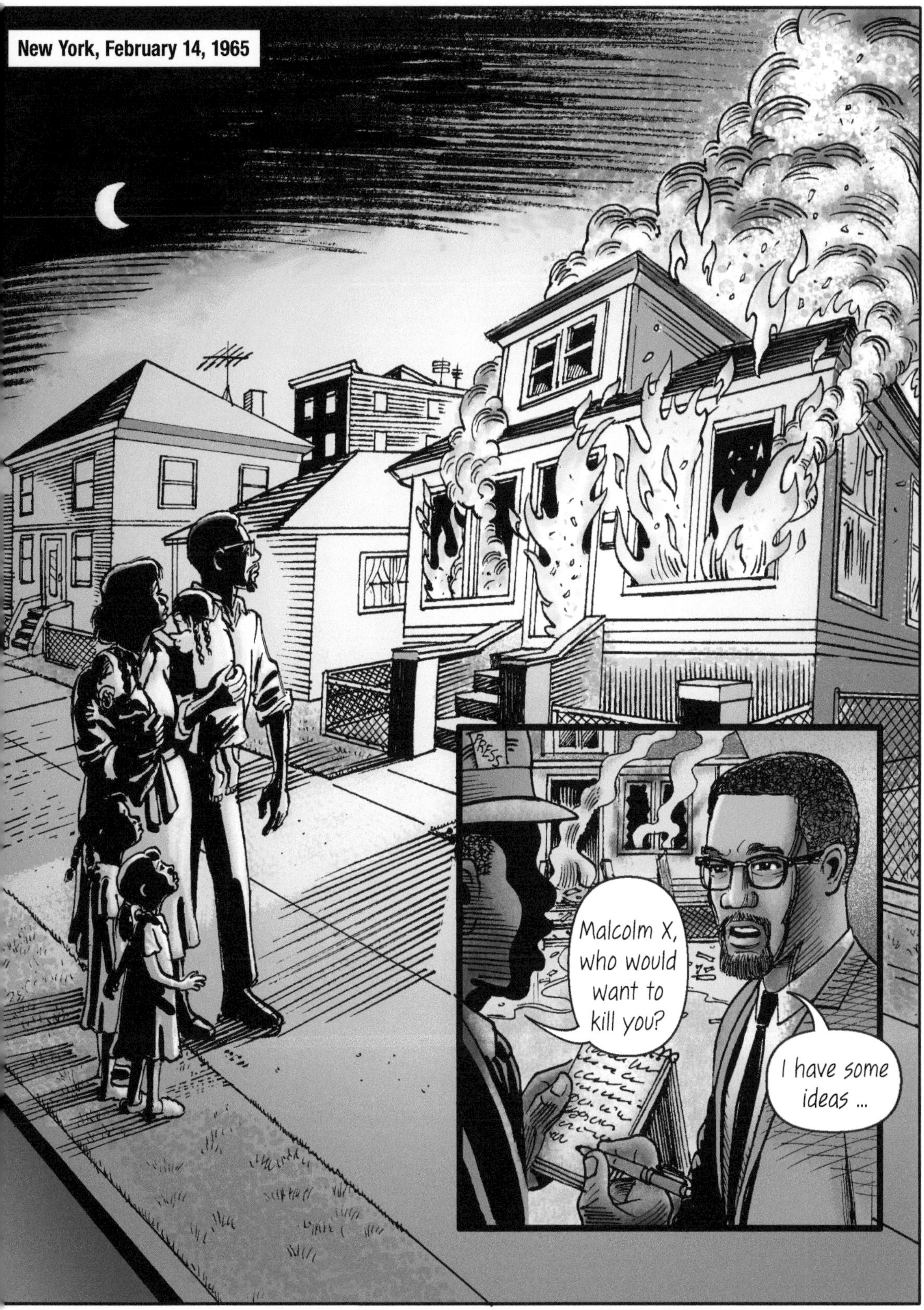
New York, February 14, 1965
PRESS
Malcolm X, who would want to kill you?
I have some ideas ...

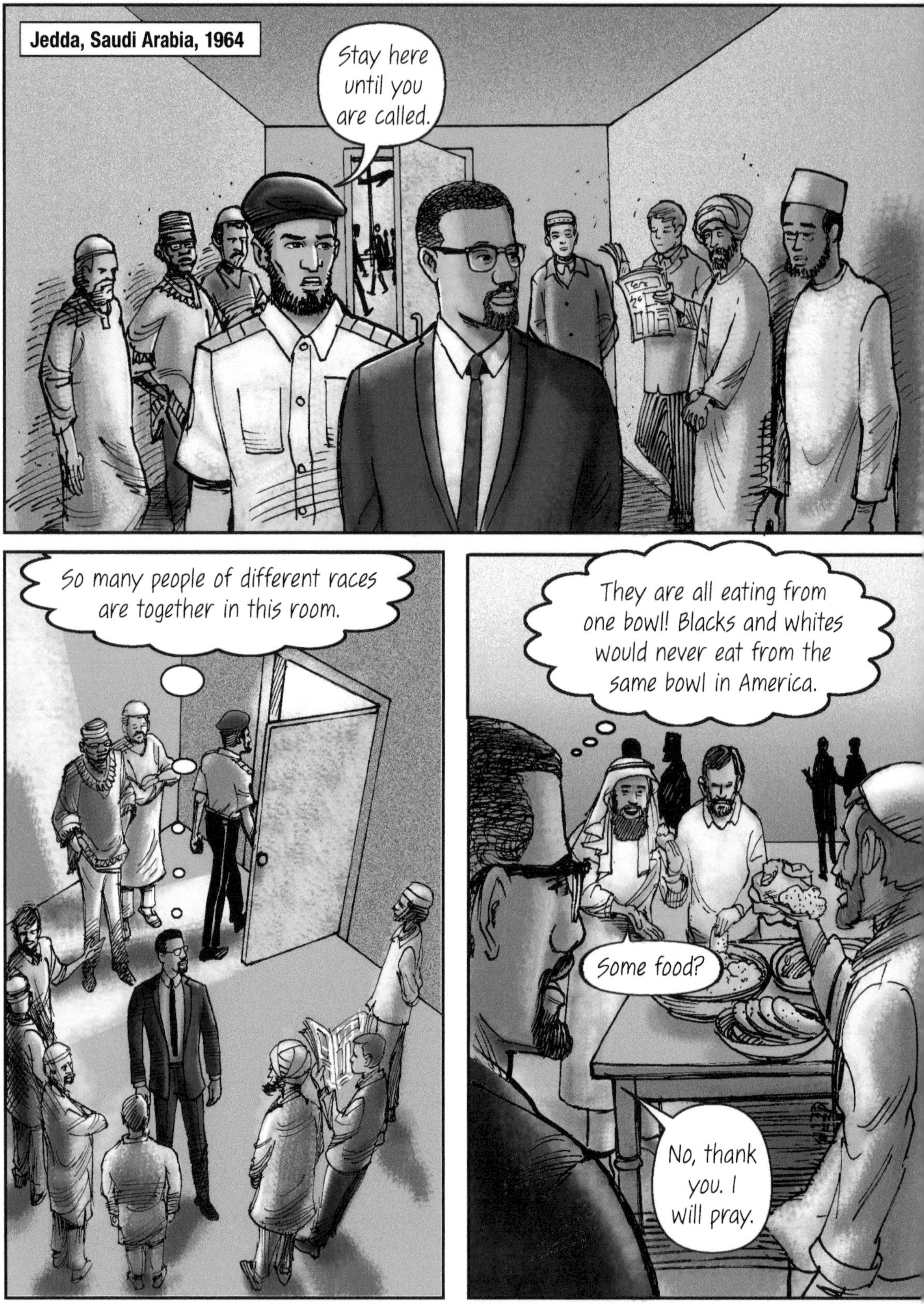
Jedda, Saudi Arabia, 1964
Stay here until you are called.
So many people of different races are together in this room.
They are all eating from one bowl! Blacks and whites would never eat from the same bowl in America.
Some food?
No, thank you. I will pray.

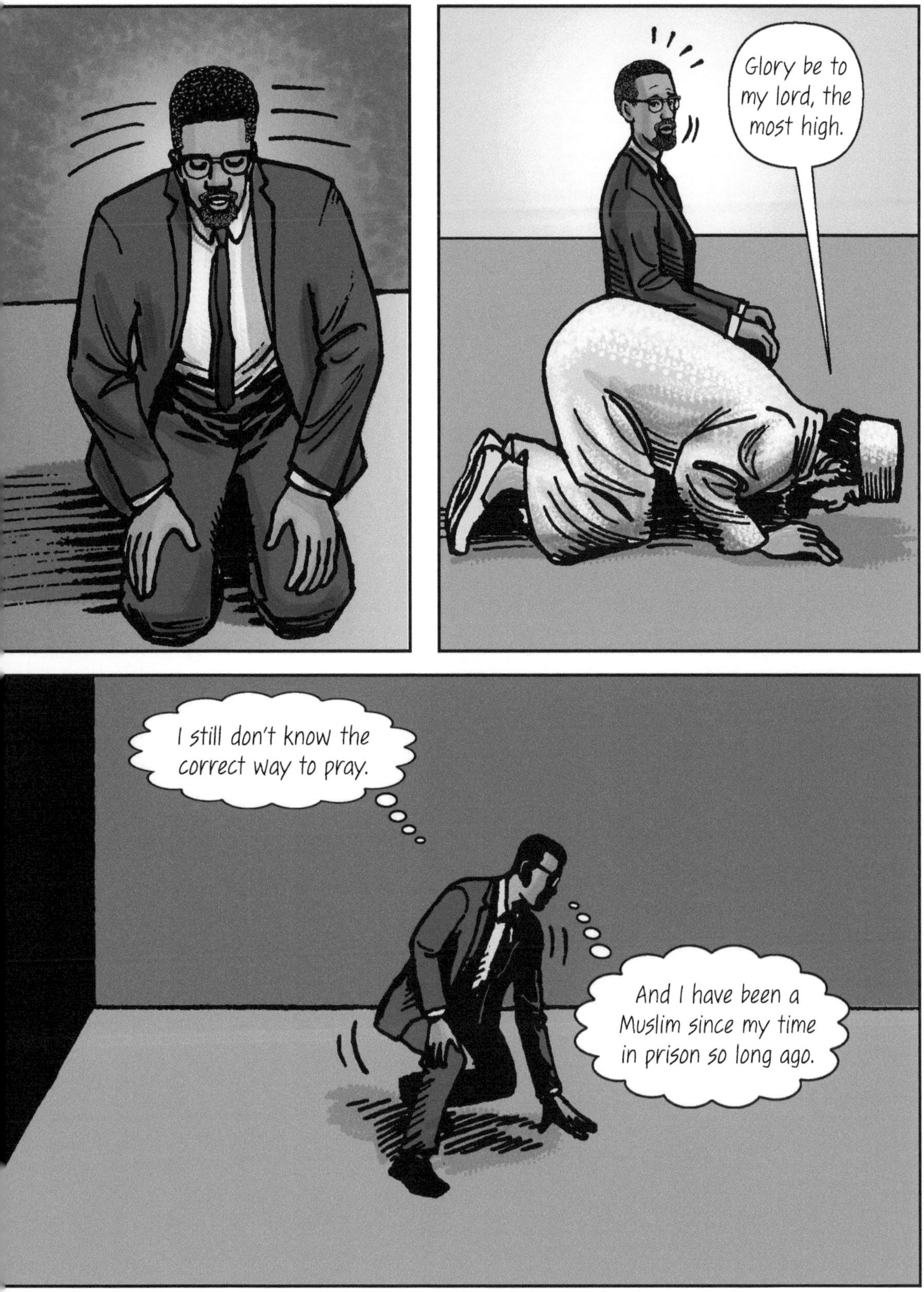
Glory be to my lord, the most high.
I still don't know the correct way to pray.
And I have been a Muslim since my time in prison so long ago.

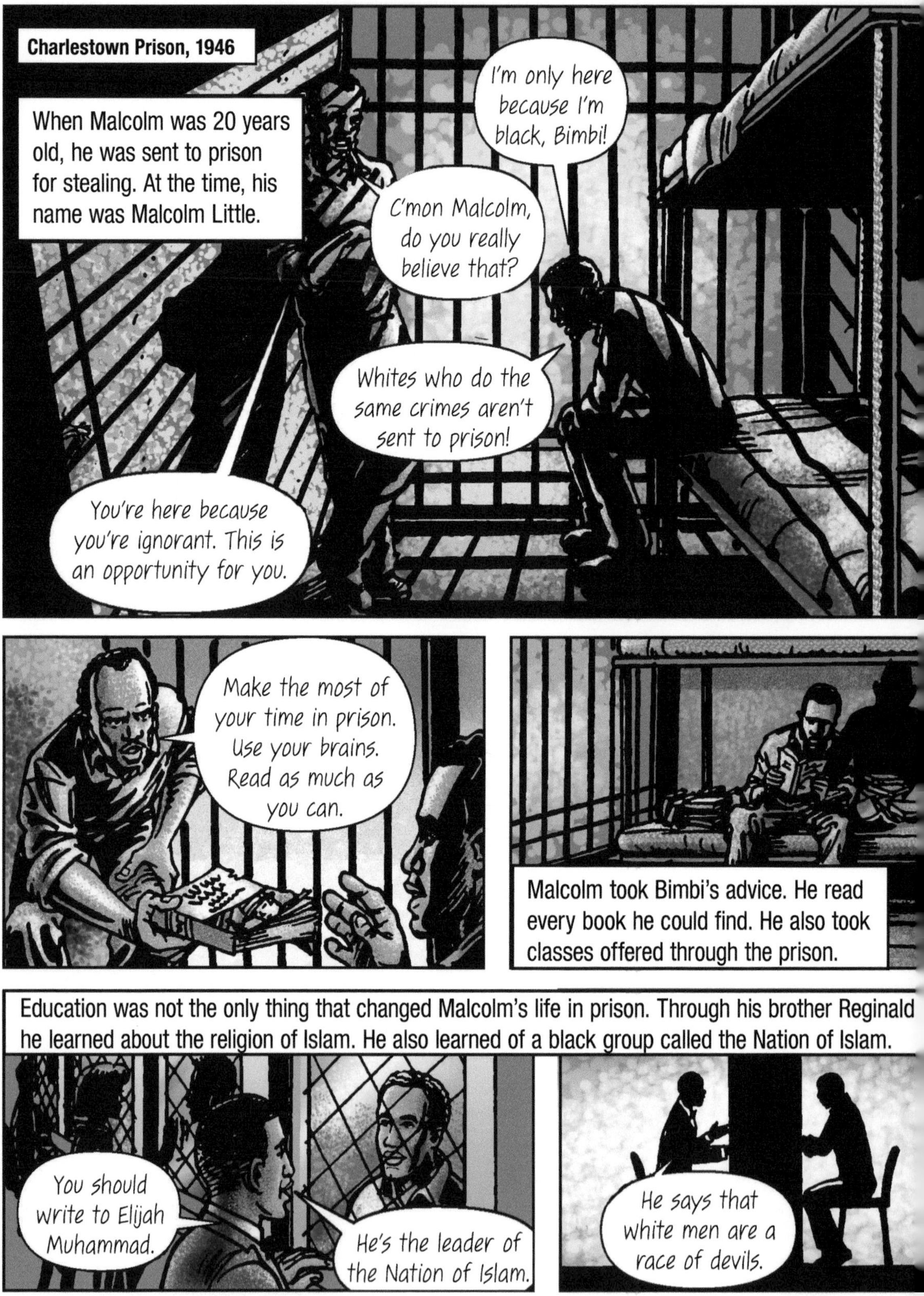
Charlestown Prison, 1946
When Malcolm was 20 years old, he was sent to prison for stealing. At the time, his name was Malcolm Little.
I'm only here because I'm black, Bimbi!
C'mon Malcolm, do you really believe that?
Whites who do the same crimes aren't sent to prison!
You're here because you're ignorant. This is an opportunity for you.
Make the most of your time in prison. Use your brains. Read as much as you can.
Malcolm took Bimbi's advice. He read every book he could find. He also took classes offered through the prison.
Education was not the only thing that changed Malcolm's life in prison. Through his brother Reginald he learned about the religion of Islam. He also learned of a black group called the Nation of Islam.
You should write to Elijah Muhammad.
He's the leader of the Nation of Islam.
He says that white men are a race of devils.

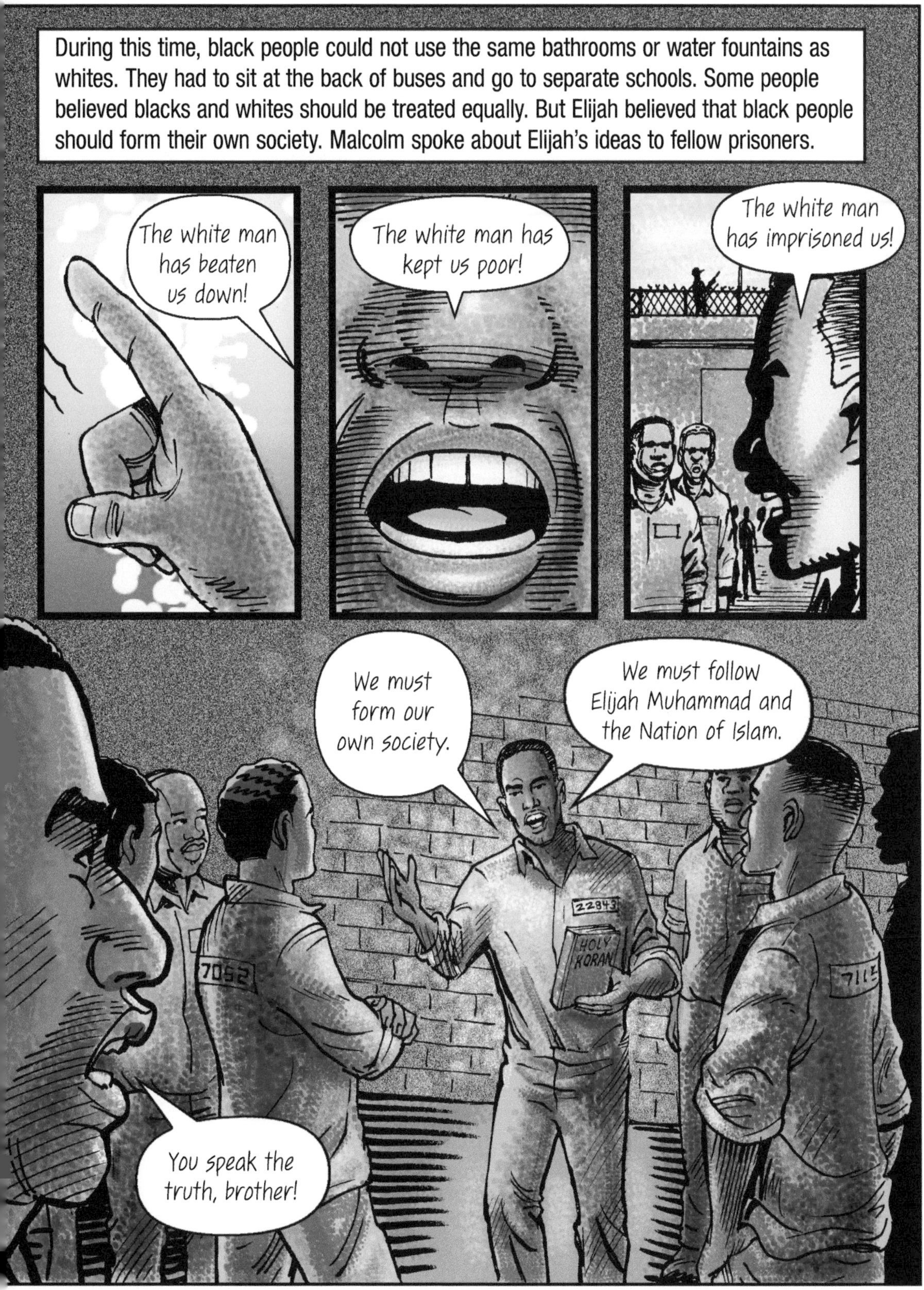
During this time, black people could not use the same bathrooms or water fountains as whites. They had to sit at the back of buses and go to separate schools. Some people believed blacks and whites should be treated equally. But Elijah believed that black people should form their own society. Malcolm spoke about Elijah's ideas to fellow prisoners.
The white man has beaten us down!
The white man has kept us poor!
The white man has imprisoned us!
We must form our own society.
We must follow Elijah Muhammad and the Nation of Islam.
22843
HOLY KORAN
7052
You speak the truth, brother!

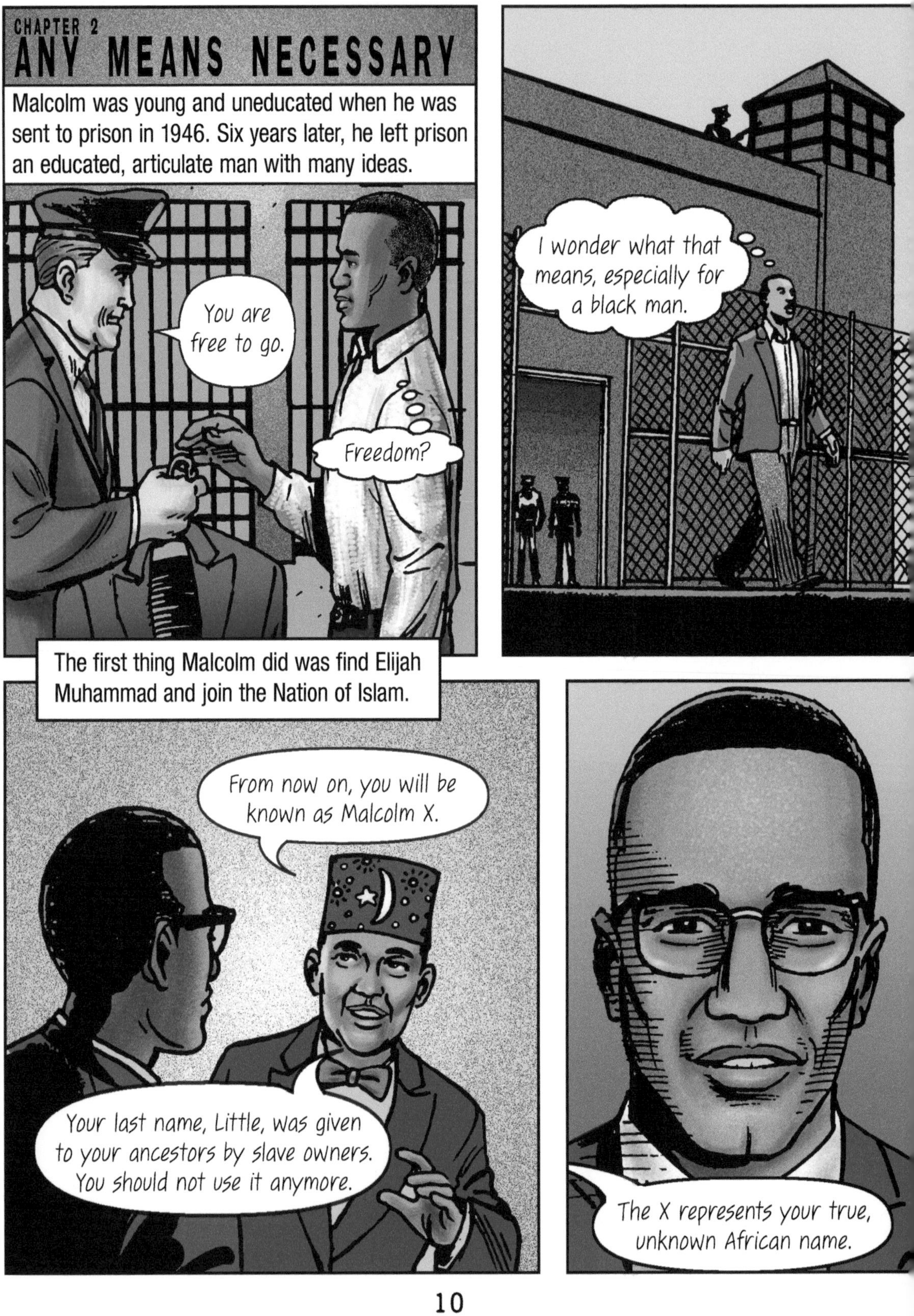
CHAPTER 2
ANY MEANS NECESSARY
Malcolm was young and uneducated when he was sent to prison in 1946. Six years later, he left prison an educated, articulate man with many ideas.
You are free to go.
Freedom?
I wonder what that means, especially for a black man.
The first thing Malcolm did was find Elijah Muhammad and join the Nation of Islam.
From now on, you will be known as Malcolm X.
Your last name, Little, was given to your ancestors by slave owners. You should not use it anymore.
The X represents your true, unknown African name.

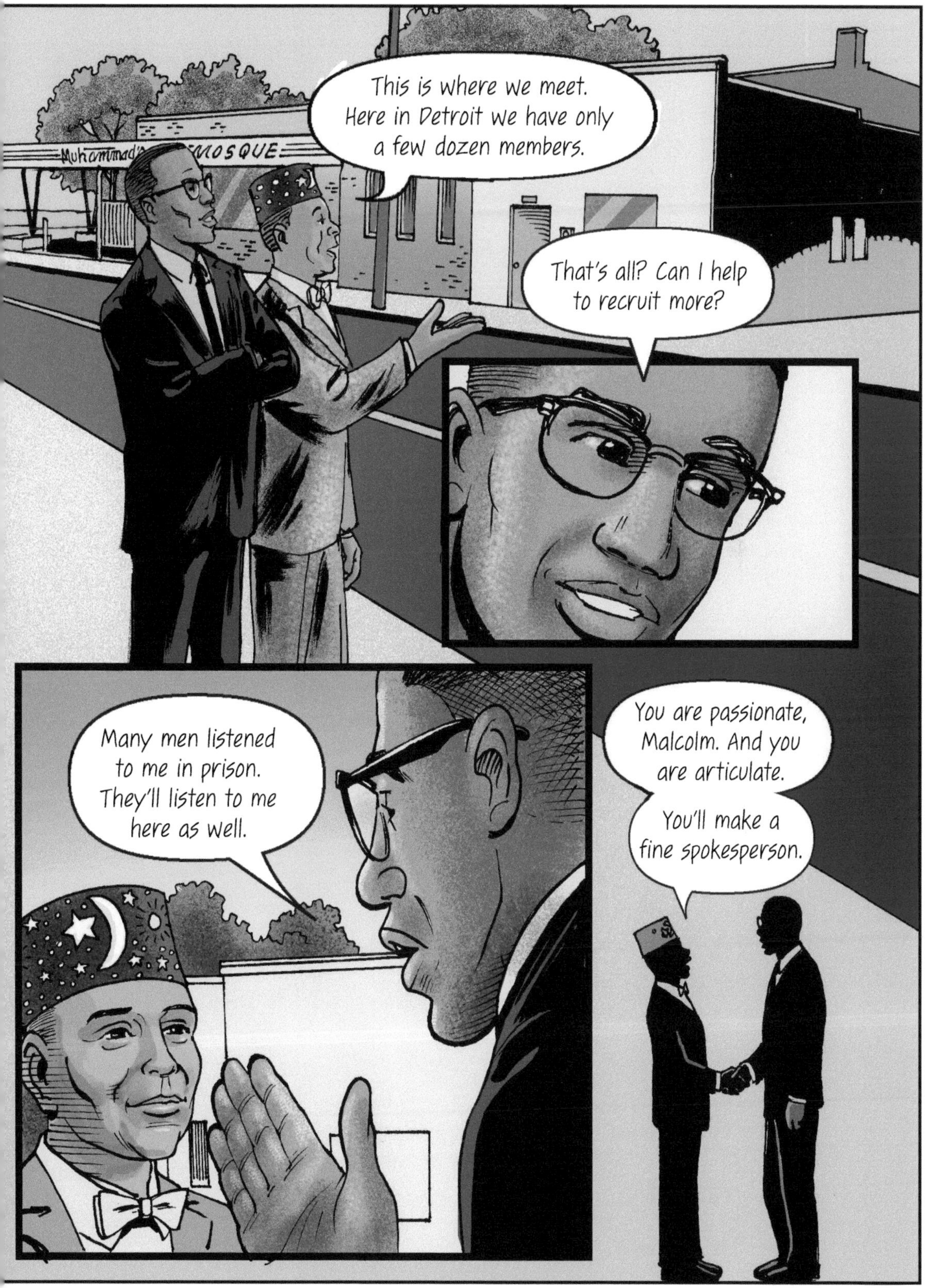

Muhammad's MOSQUE
This is where we meet. Here in Detroit we have only a few dozen members.
That's all? Can I help to recruit more?
Many men listened to me in prison. They'll listen to me here as well.
You are passionate, Malcolm. And you are articulate.
You'll make a fine spokesperson.

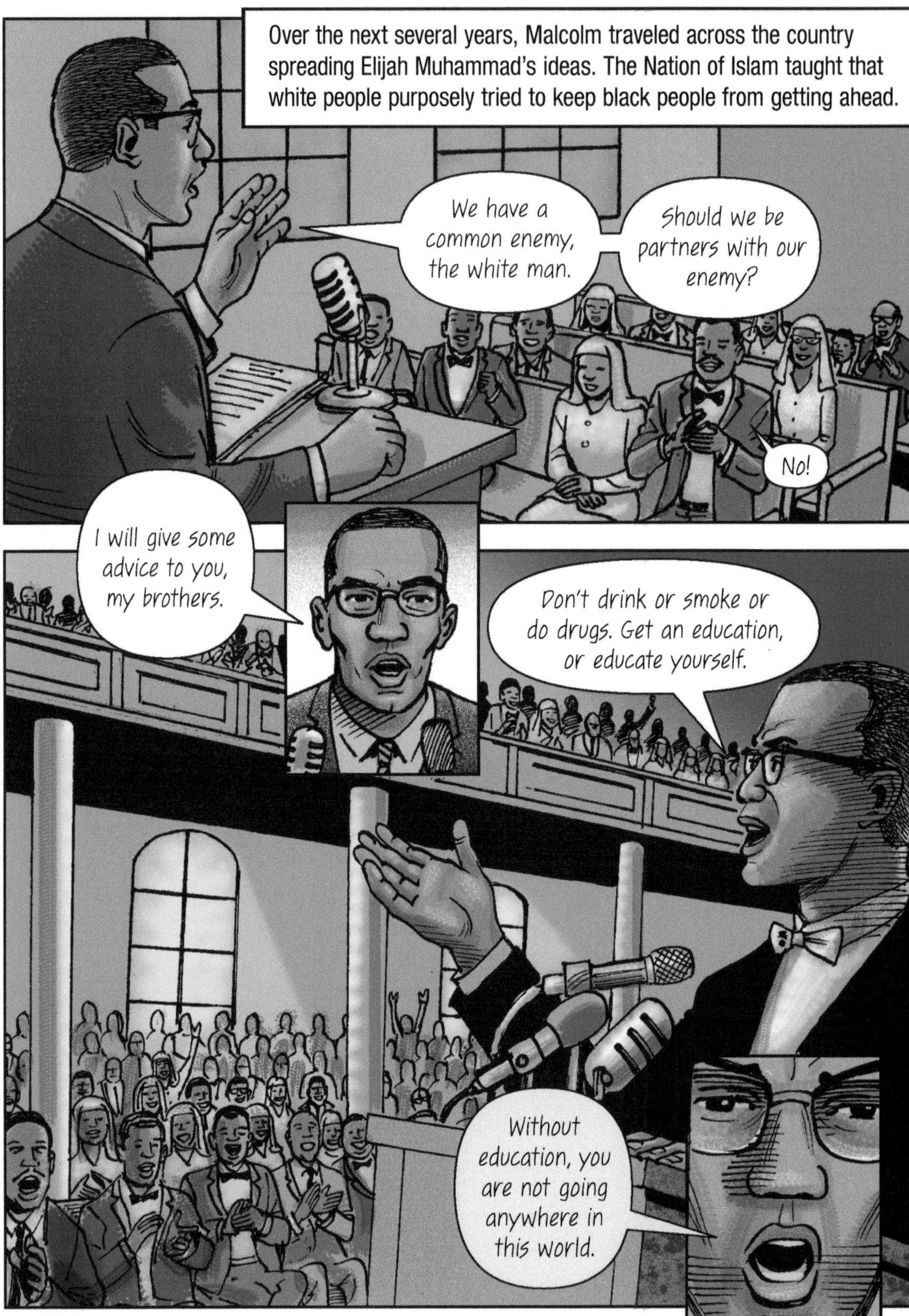
Over the next several years, Malcolm traveled across the country spreading Elijah Muhammad's ideas. The Nation of Islam taught that white people purposely tried to keep black people from getting ahead.
We have a common enemy, the white man.
Should we be partners with our enemy?
No!
I will give some advice to you, my brothers.
Don't drink or smoke or do drugs. Get an education, or educate yourself.
Without education, you are not going anywhere in this world.

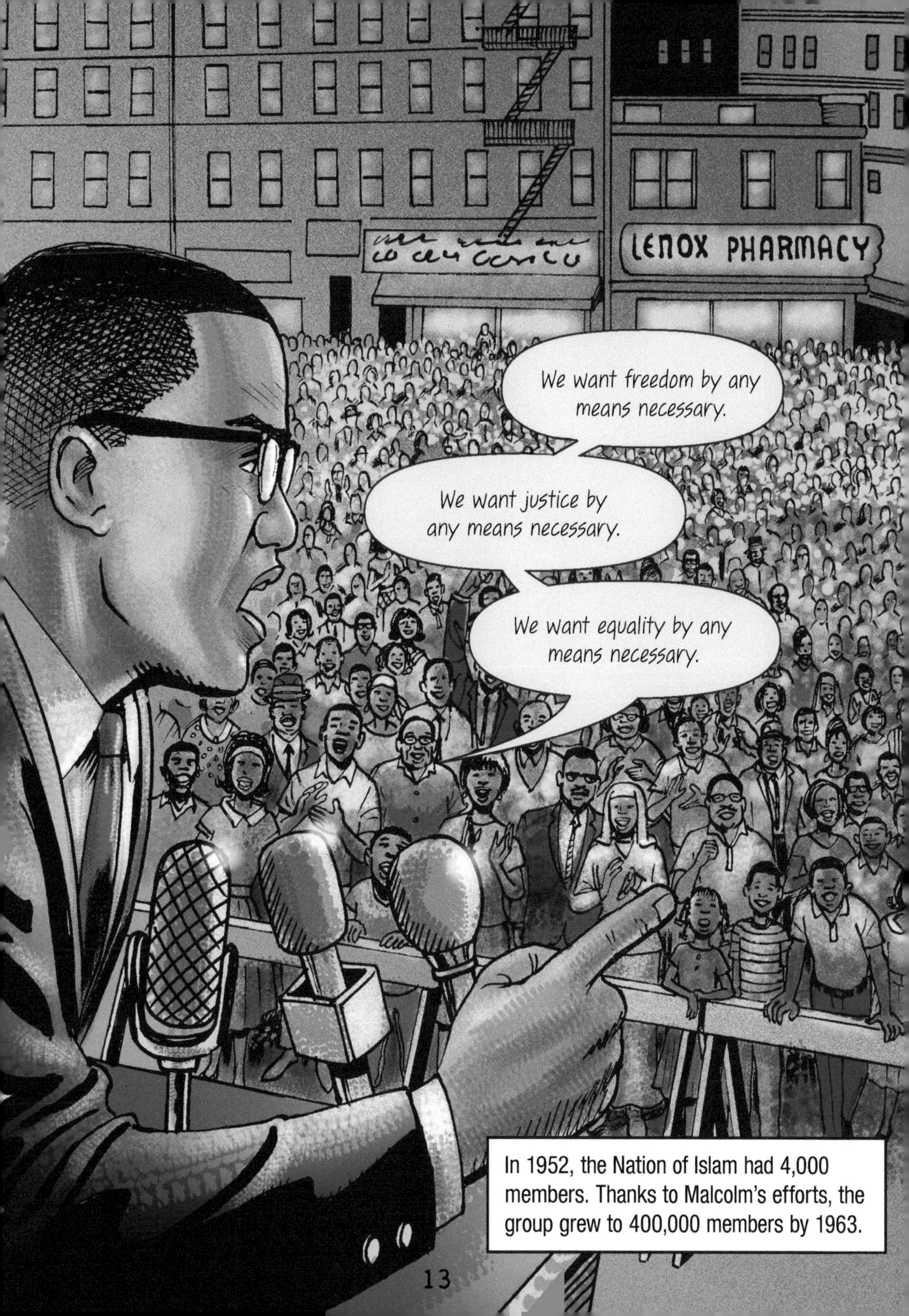
LENOX PHARMACY
We want freedom by any means necessary.
We want justice by any means necessary.
We want equality by any means necessary.

In 1952, the Nation of Islam had 4,000 members. Thanks to Malcolm's efforts, the group grew to 400,000 members by 1963.

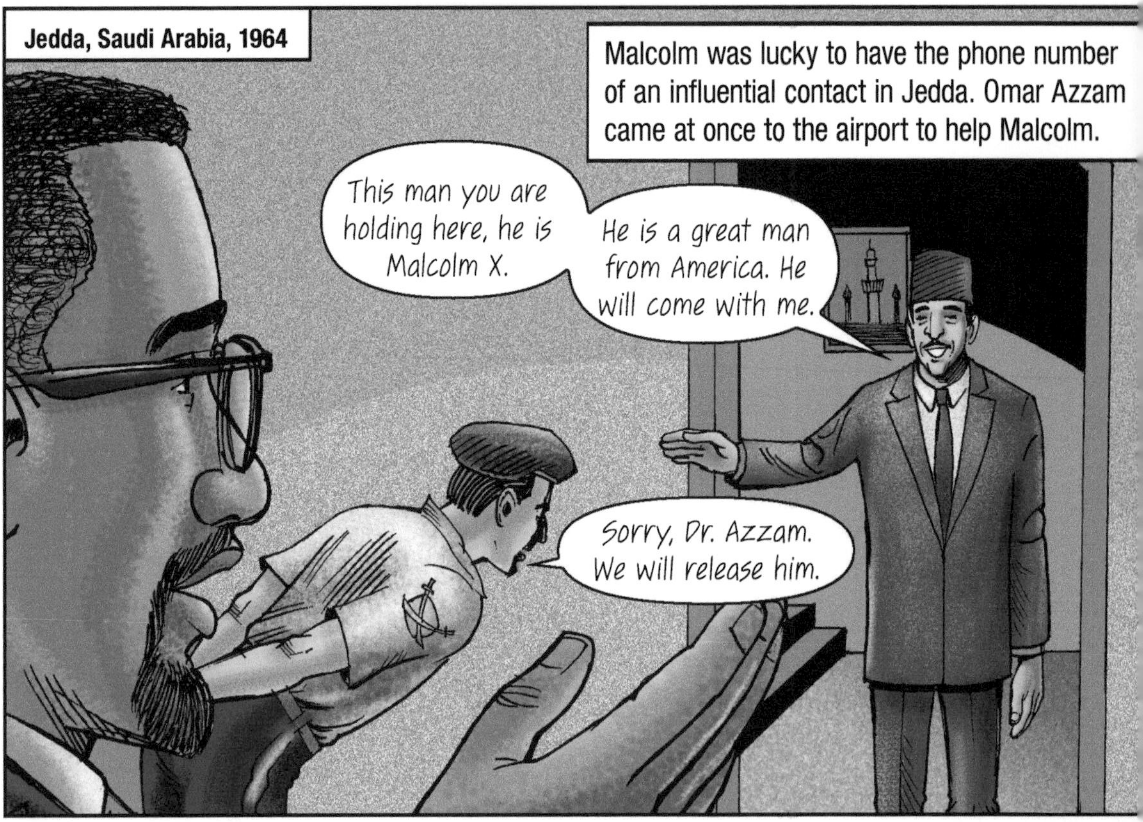
Jedda, Saudi Arabia, 1964
Malcolm was lucky to have the phone number of an influential contact in Jedda. Omar Azzam came at once to the airport to help Malcolm.
This man you are holding here, he is Malcolm X.
He is a great man from America. He will come with me.
Sorry, Dr. Azzam. We will release him.

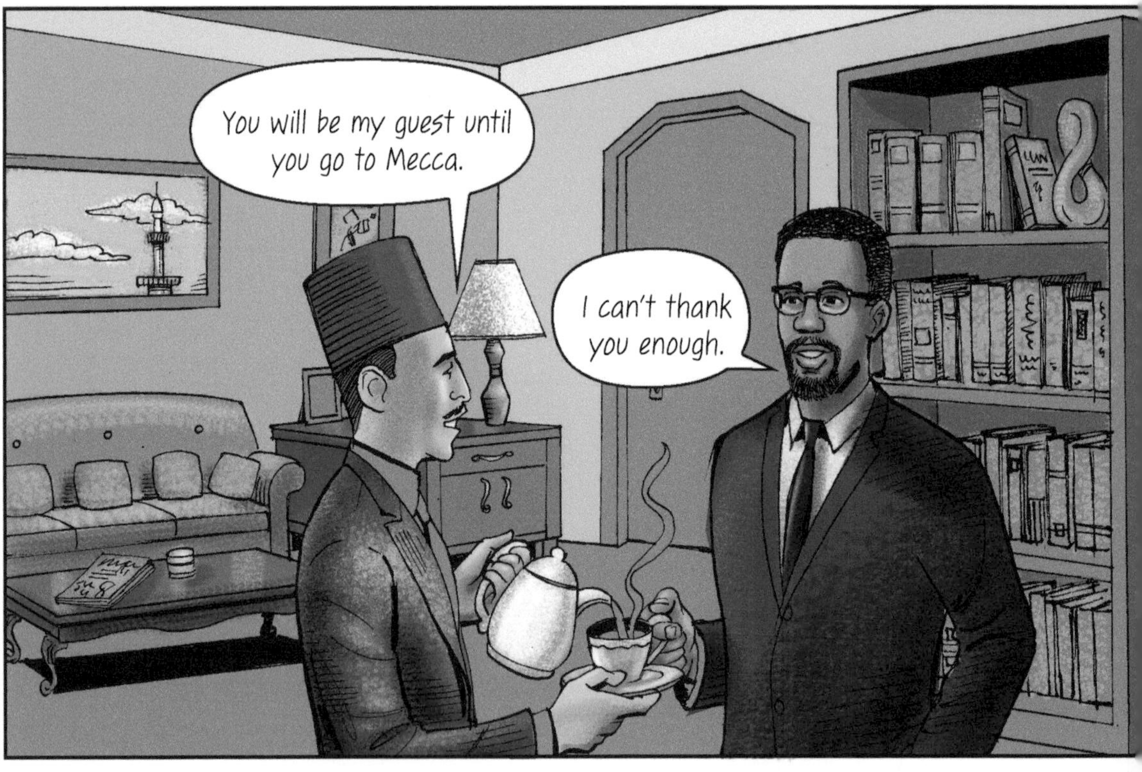
You will be my guest until you go to Mecca.
I can't thank you enough.

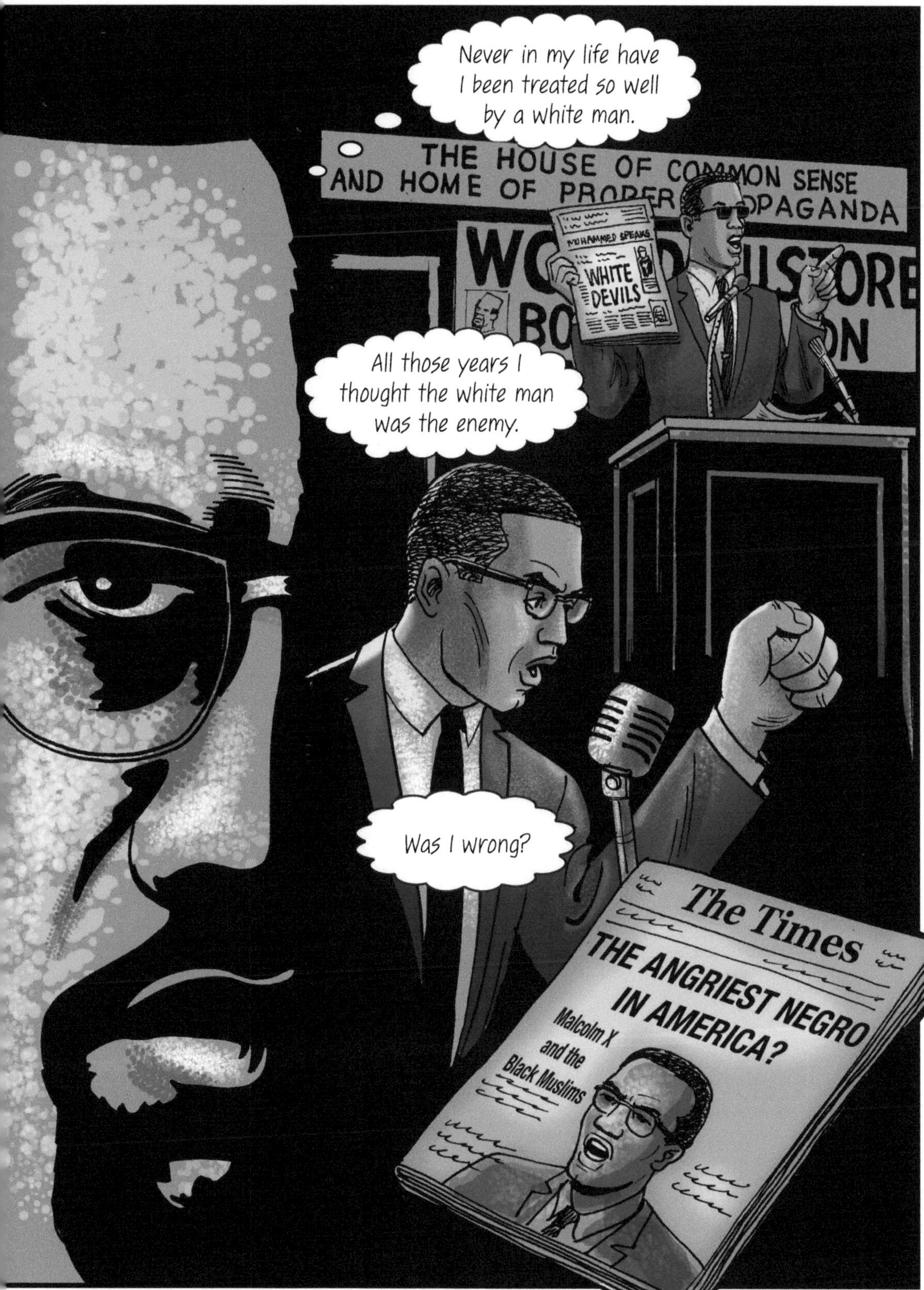
Never in my life have I been treated so well by a white man.
THE HOUSE OF COMMON SENSE AND HOME OF PROPER PROPAGANDA
MUHAMMED SPEAKS
WHITE DEVILS
All those years I thought the white man was the enemy.
Was I wrong?
The Times
THE ANGRIEST NEGRO IN AMERICA?
Malcolm X and the Black Muslims

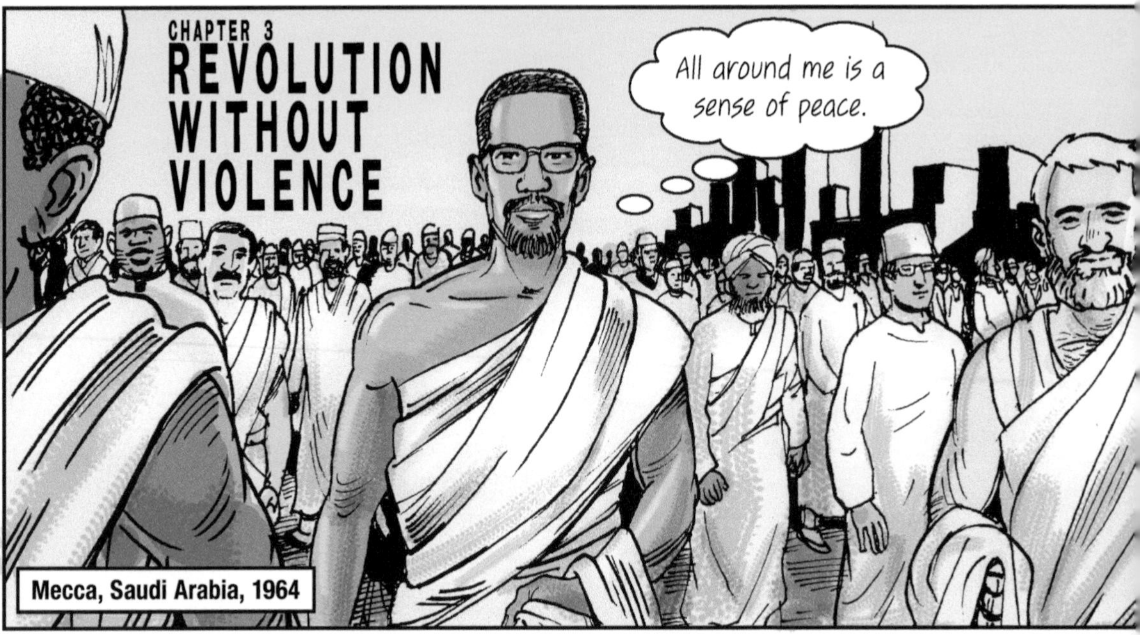
CHAPTER 3
REVOLUTION WITHOUT VIOLENCE
All around me is a sense of peace.
Mecca, Saudi Arabia, 1964

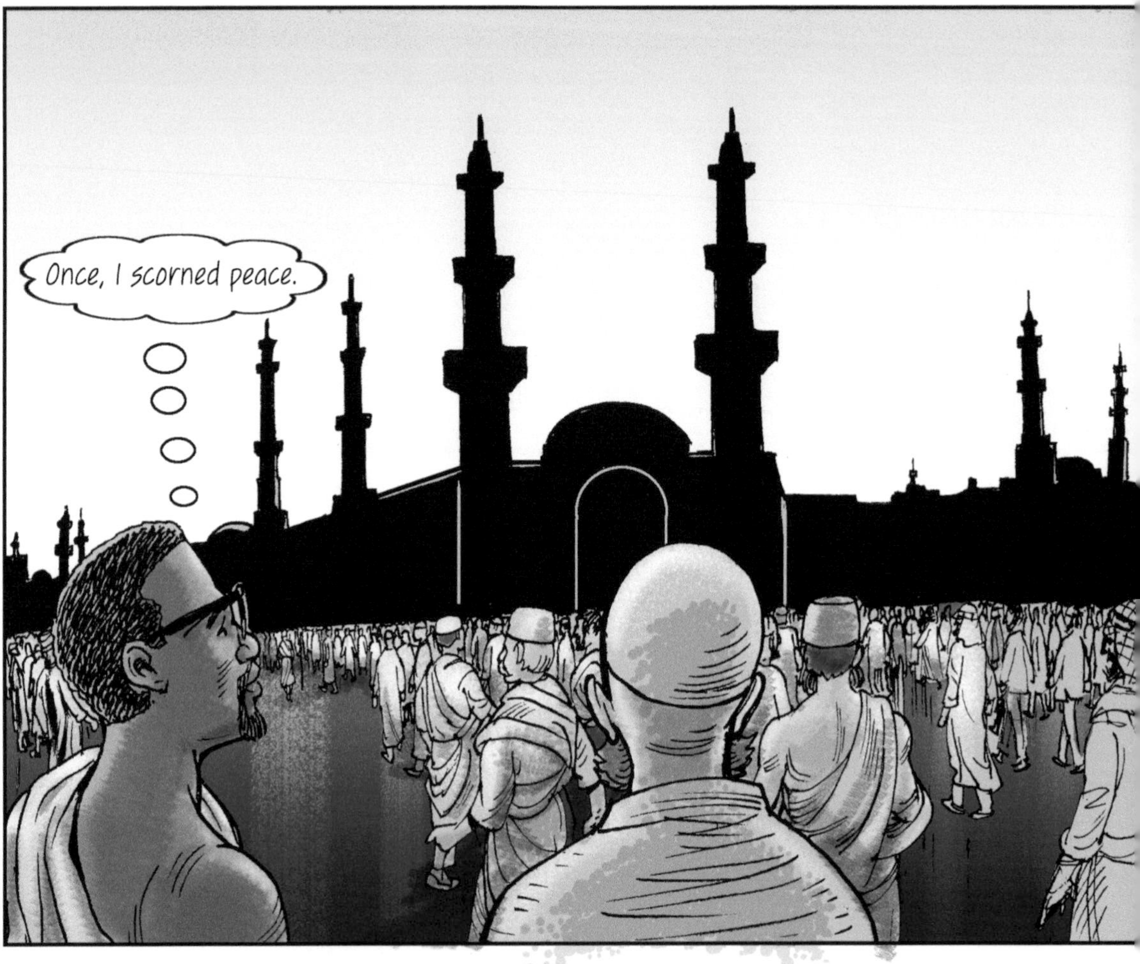
Once, I scorned peace.

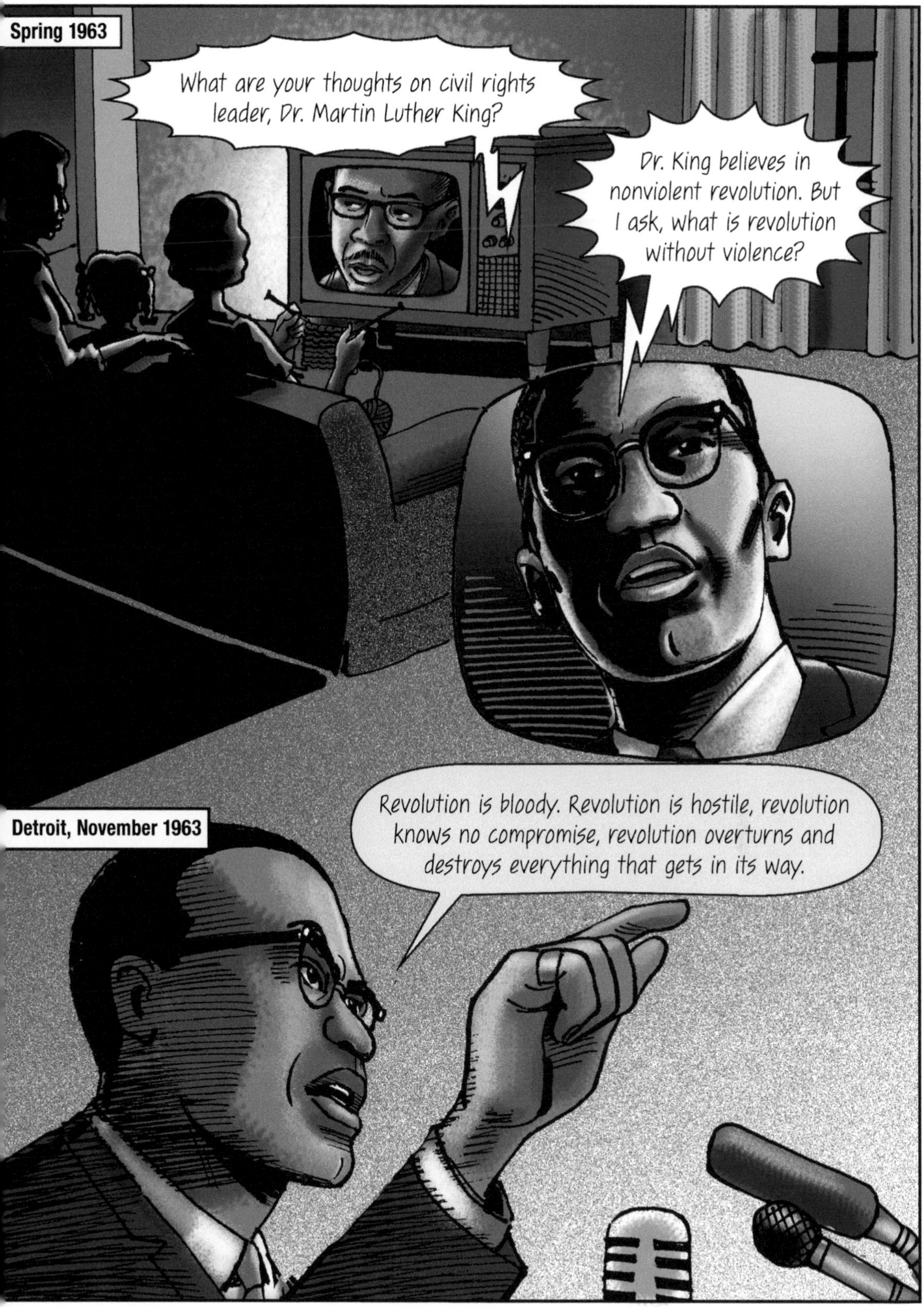
Spring 1963
What are your thoughts on civil rights leader, Dr. Martin Luther King?
Dr. King believes in nonviolent revolution. But I ask, what is revolution without violence?
Detroit, November 1963
Revolution is bloody. Revolution is hostile, revolution knows no compromise, revolution overturns and destroys everything that gets in its way.

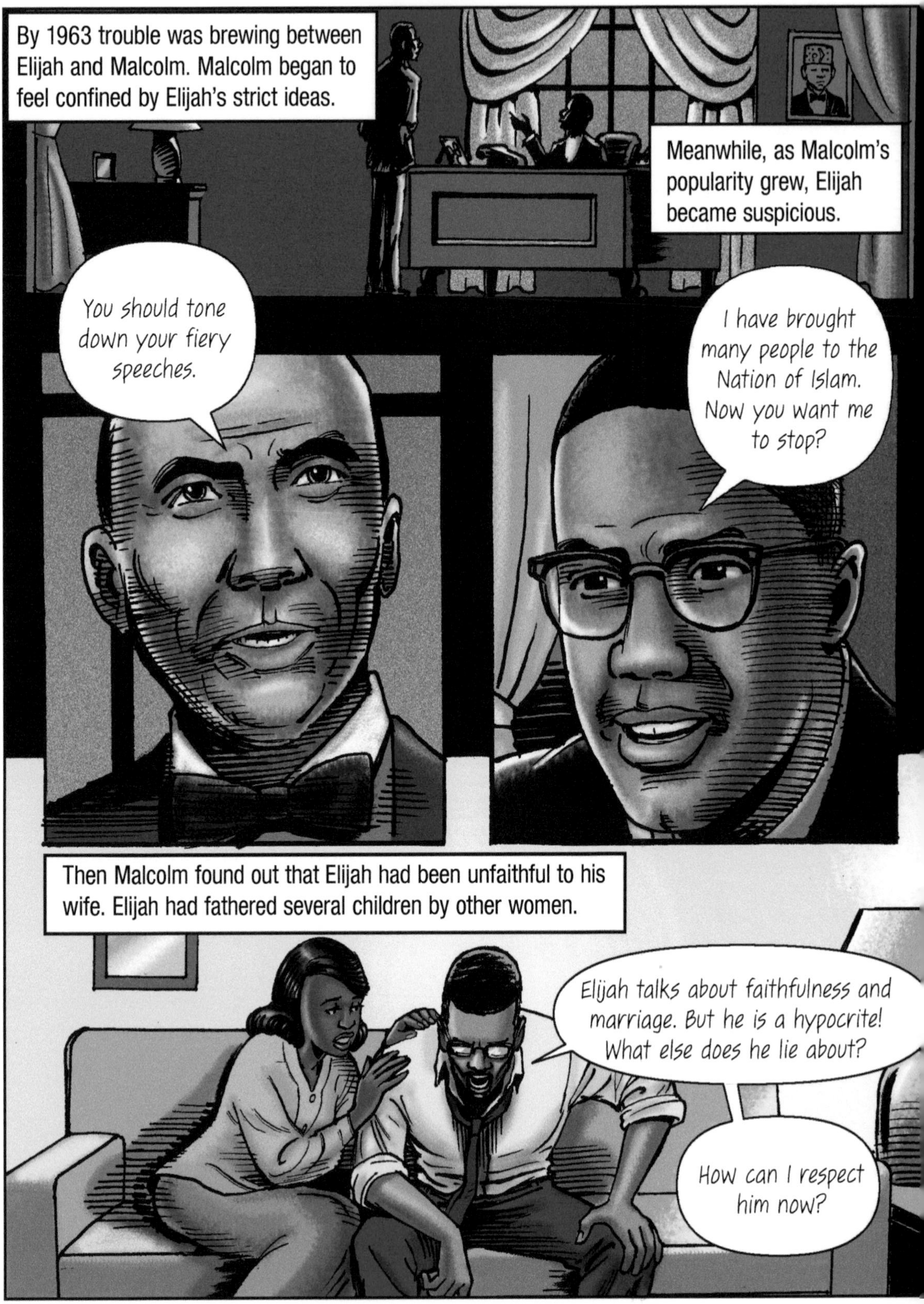

By 1963 trouble was brewing between Elijah and Malcolm. Malcolm began to feel confined by Elijah's strict ideas.
Meanwhile, as Malcolm's popularity grew, Elijah became suspicious.
You should tone down your fiery speeches.
I have brought many people to the Nation of Islam. Now you want me to stop?
Then Malcolm found out that Elijah had been unfaithful to his wife. Elijah had fathered several children by other women.
Elijah talks about faithfulness and marriage. But he is a hypocrite! What else does he lie about?
How can I respect him now?

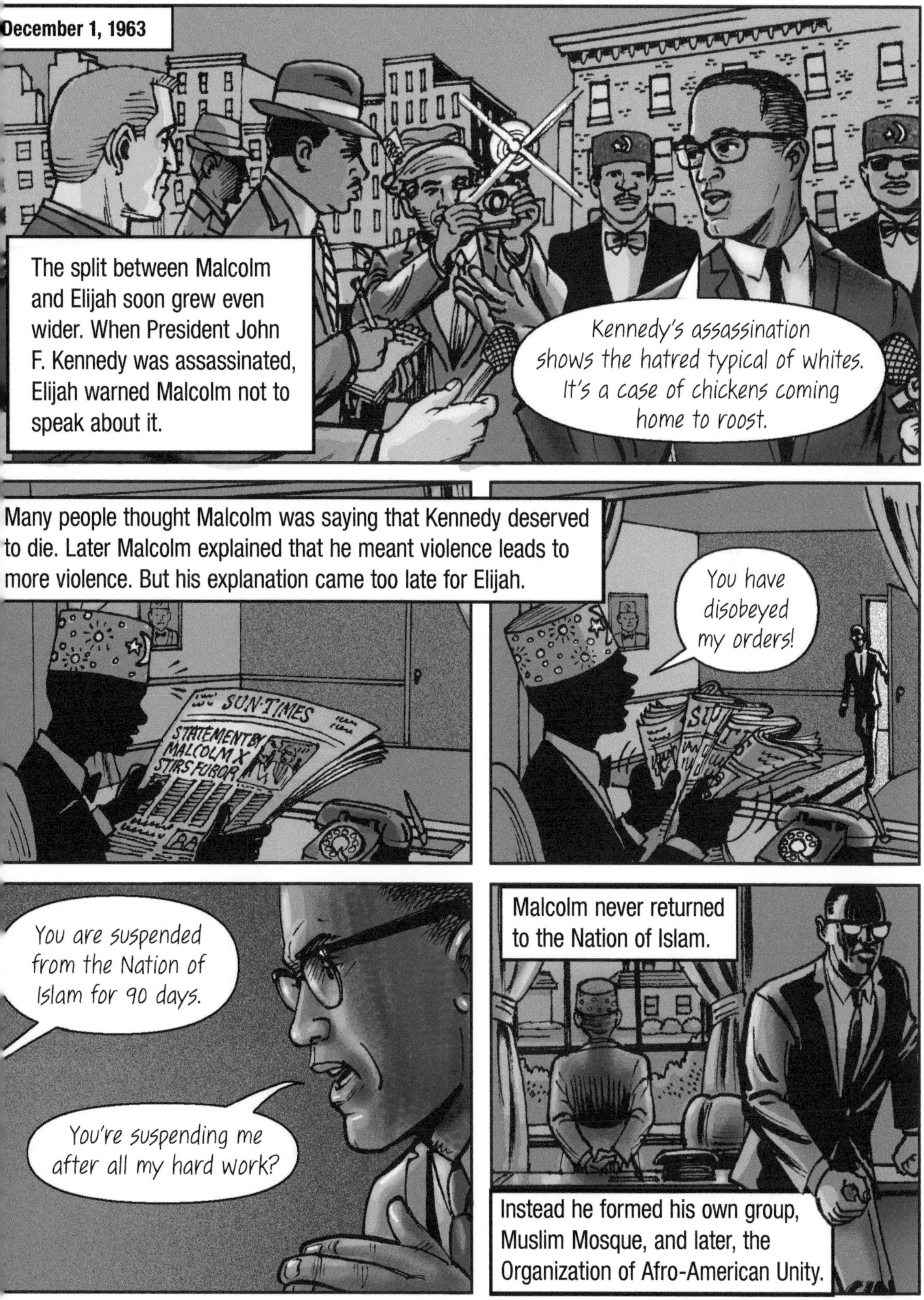
December 1, 1963
The split between Malcolm and Elijah soon grew even wider. When President John F. Kennedy was assassinated, Elijah warned Malcolm not to speak about it.
Kennedy's assassination shows the hatred typical of whites. It's a case of chickens coming home to roost.
Many people thought Malcolm was saying that Kennedy deserved to die. Later Malcolm explained that he meant violence leads to more violence. But his explanation came too late for Elijah.
SUN-TIMES
STATEMENT BY MALCOLM X STIRS FUROR
You have disobeyed my orders!
You are suspended from the Nation of Islam for 90 days.
You're suspending me after all my hard work?
Malcolm never returned to the Nation of Islam.
Instead he formed his own group, Muslim Mosque, and later, the Organization of Afro-American Unity.

CHAPTER 3
SHINING PRINCE

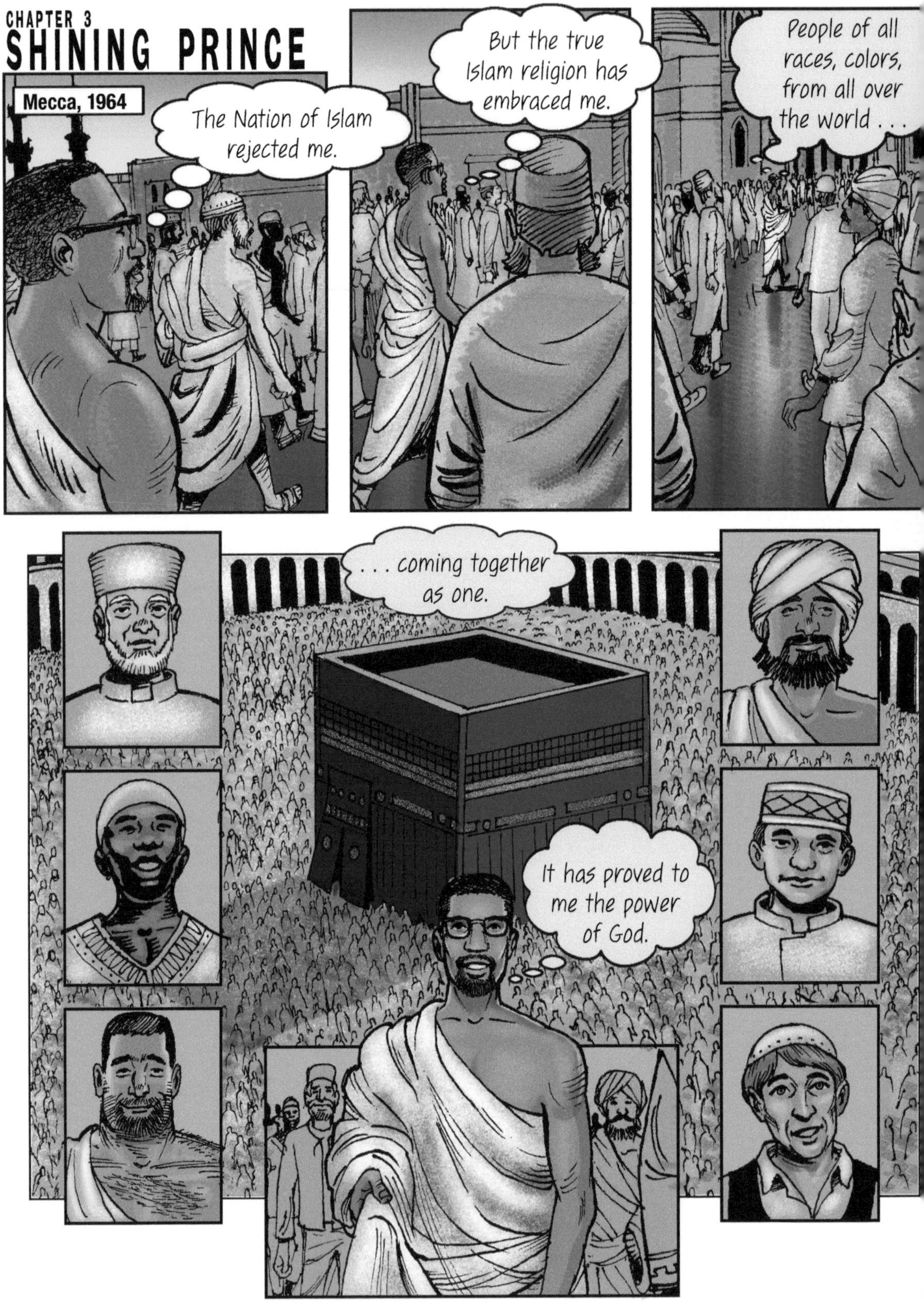
Mecca, 1964
The Nation of Islam rejected me.
But the true Islam religion has embraced me.
People of all races, colors, from all over the world . . .
. . . coming together as one.
It has proved to me the power of God.

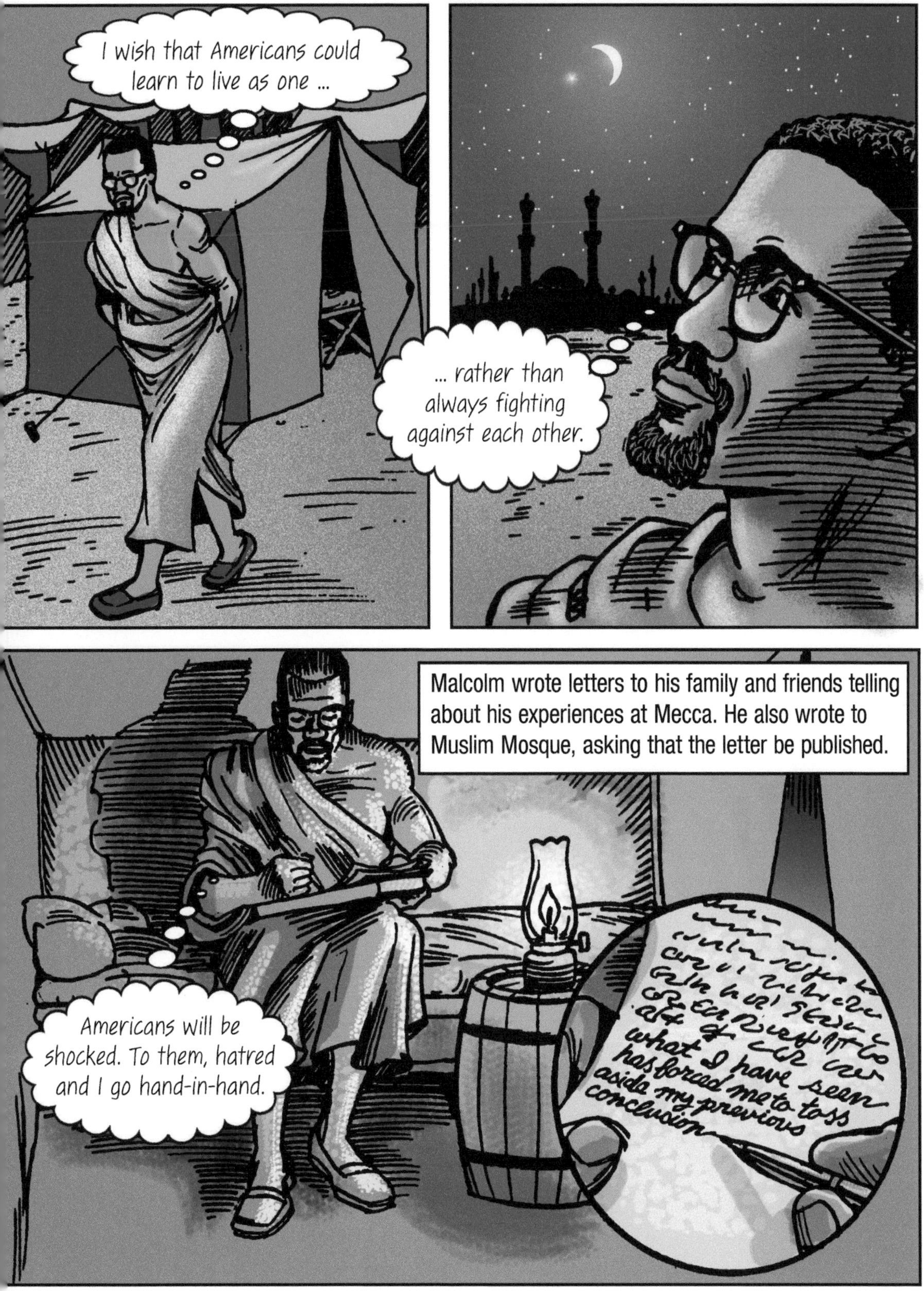
I wish that Americans could learn to live as one ...
... rather than always fighting against each other.
Malcolm wrote letters to his family and friends telling about his experiences at Mecca. He also wrote to Muslim Mosque, asking that the letter be published.
Americans will be shocked. To them, hatred and I go hand-in-hand.
what I have seen
has forced me to toss
aside my previous
conclusion

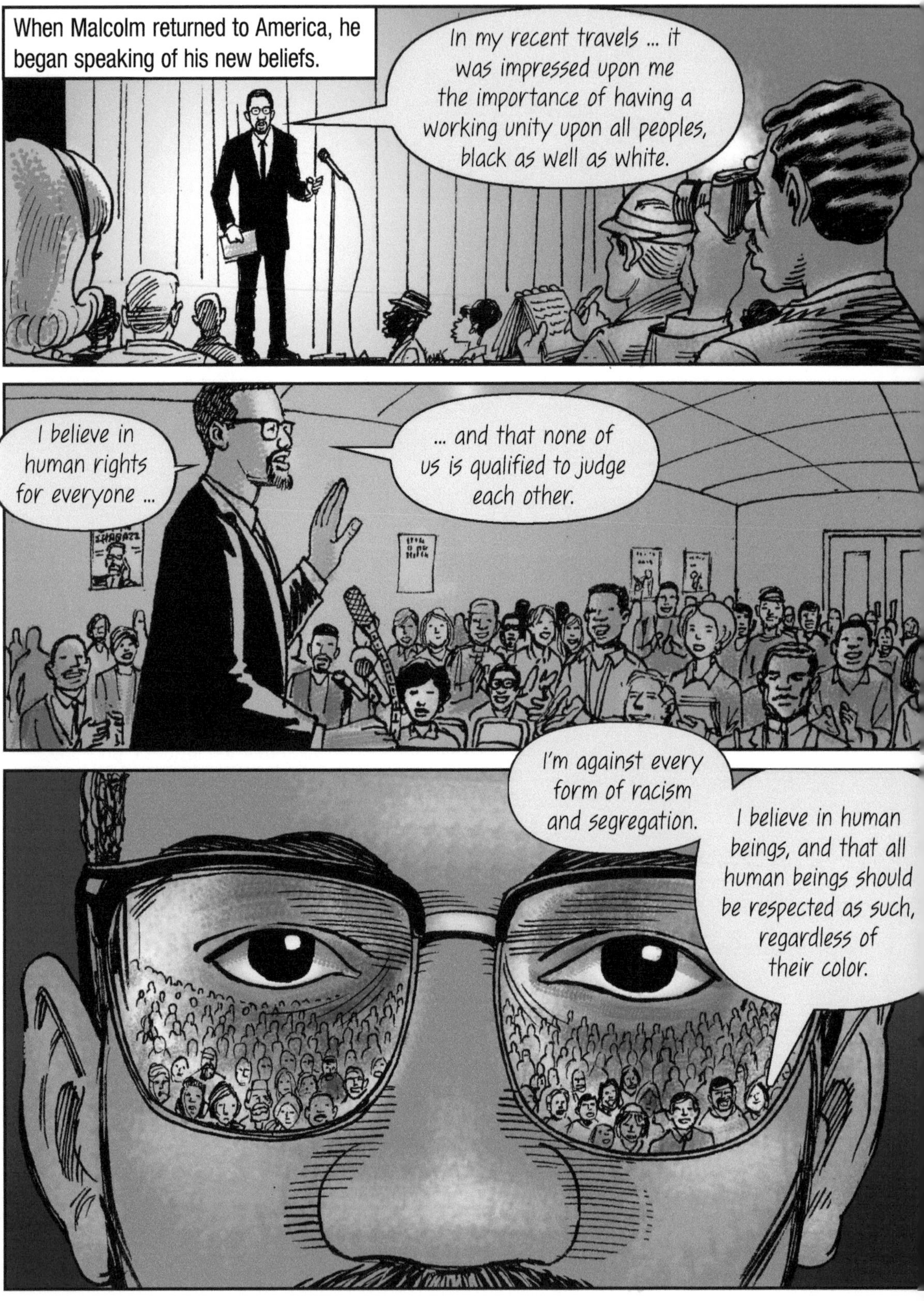
When Malcolm returned to America, he began speaking of his new beliefs.
In my recent travels ... it was impressed upon me the importance of having a working unity upon all peoples, black as well as white.
I believe in human rights for everyone ...
... and that none of us is qualified to judge each other.
I'm against every form of racism and segregation.
I believe in human beings, and that all human beings should be respected as such, regardless of their color.

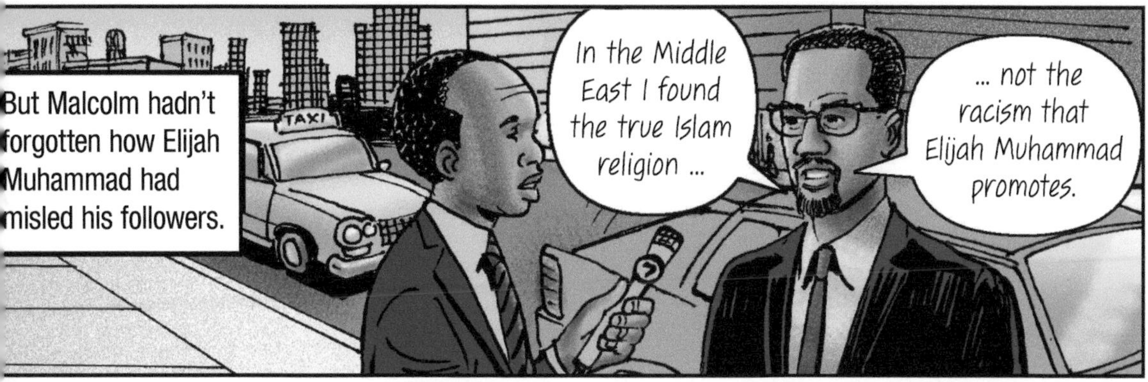
But Malcolm hadn't forgotten how Elijah Muhammad had misled his followers.
TAXI
In the Middle East I found the true Islam religion ...
... not the racism that Elijah Muhammad promotes.

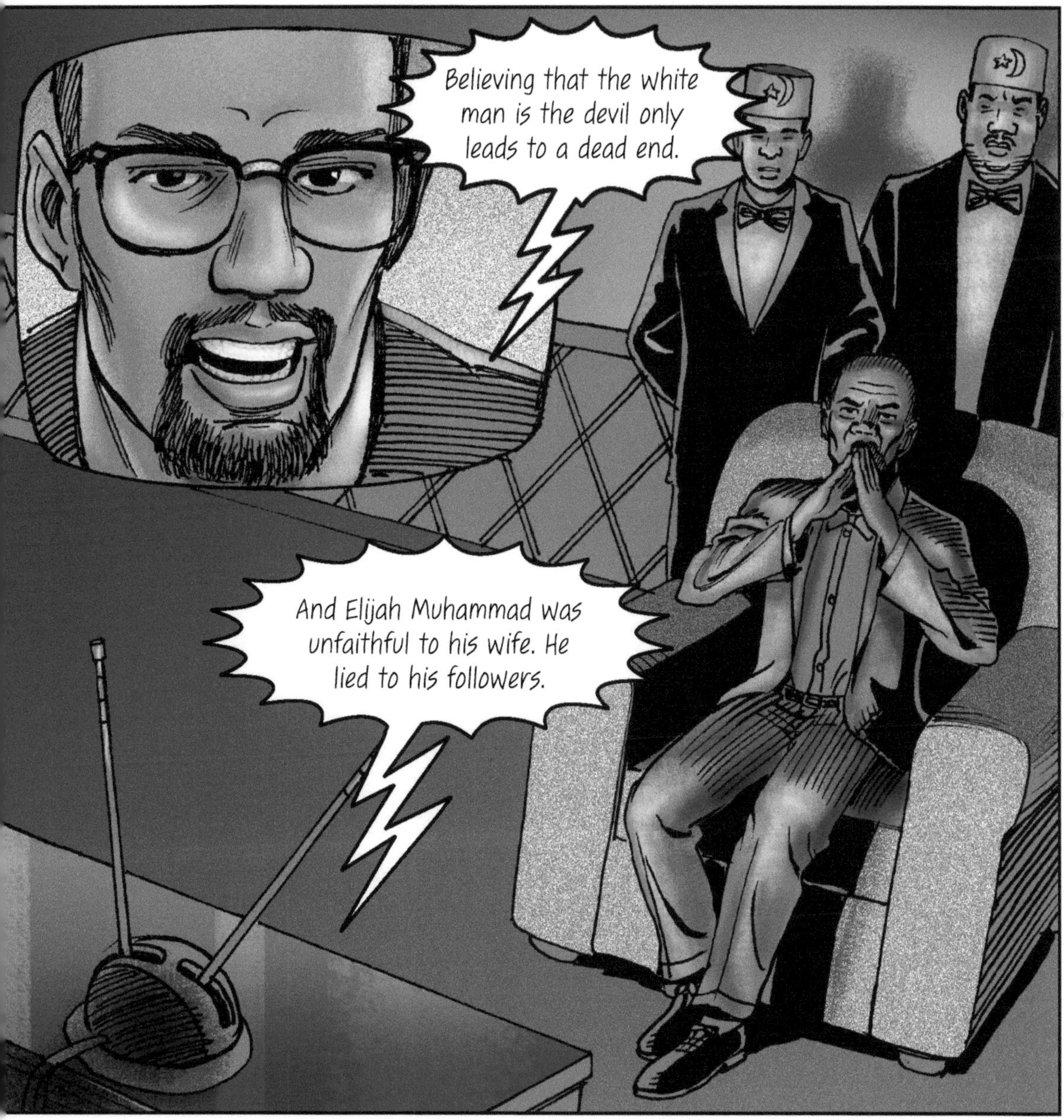
Believing that the white man is the devil only leads to a dead end.
And Elijah Muhammad was unfaithful to his wife. He lied to his followers.

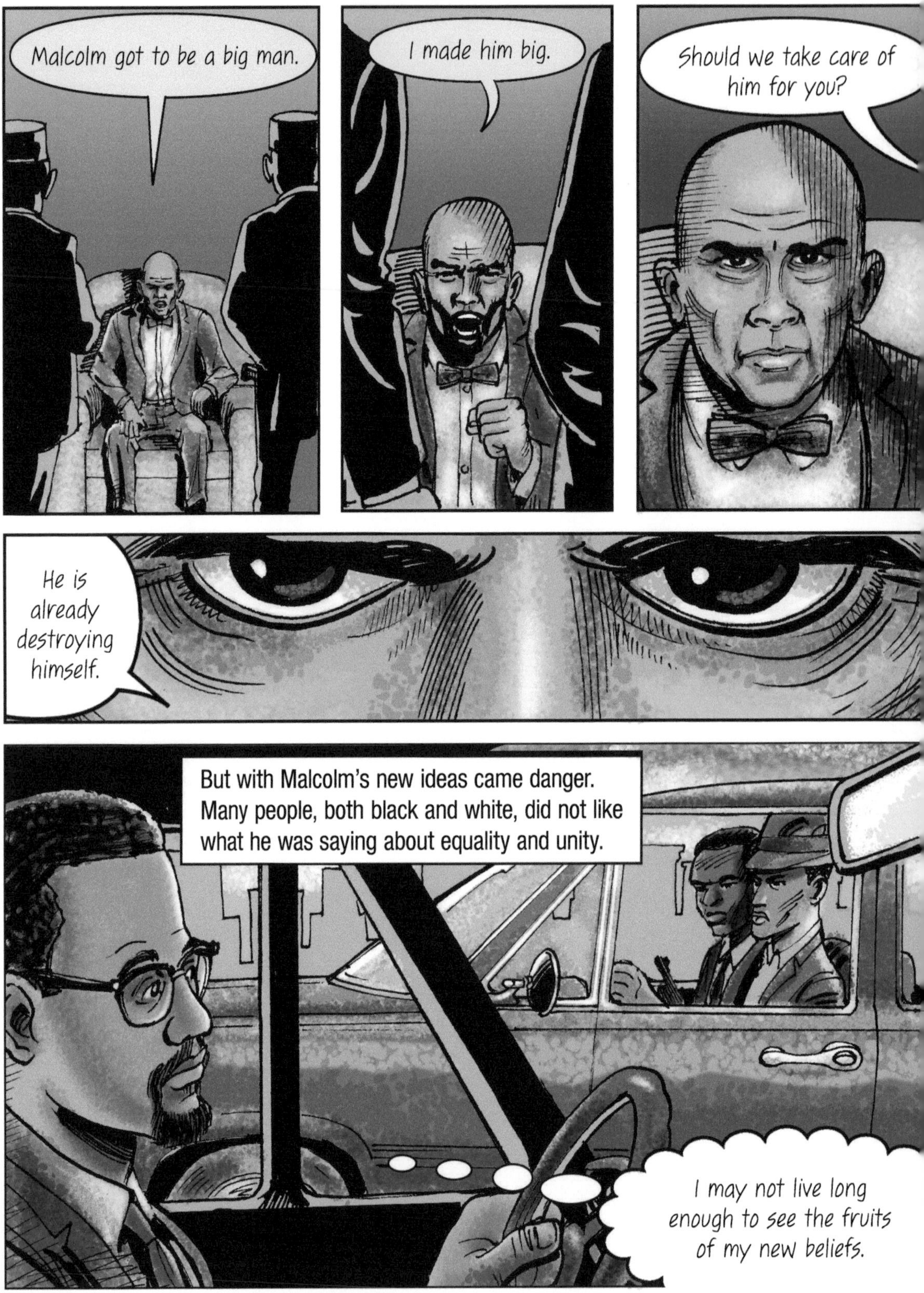
Malcolm got to be a big man.
I made him big.
Should we take care of him for you?
He is already destroying himself.
But with Malcolm's new ideas came danger. Many people, both black and white, did not like what he was saying about equality and unity.
I may not live long enough to see the fruits of my new beliefs.

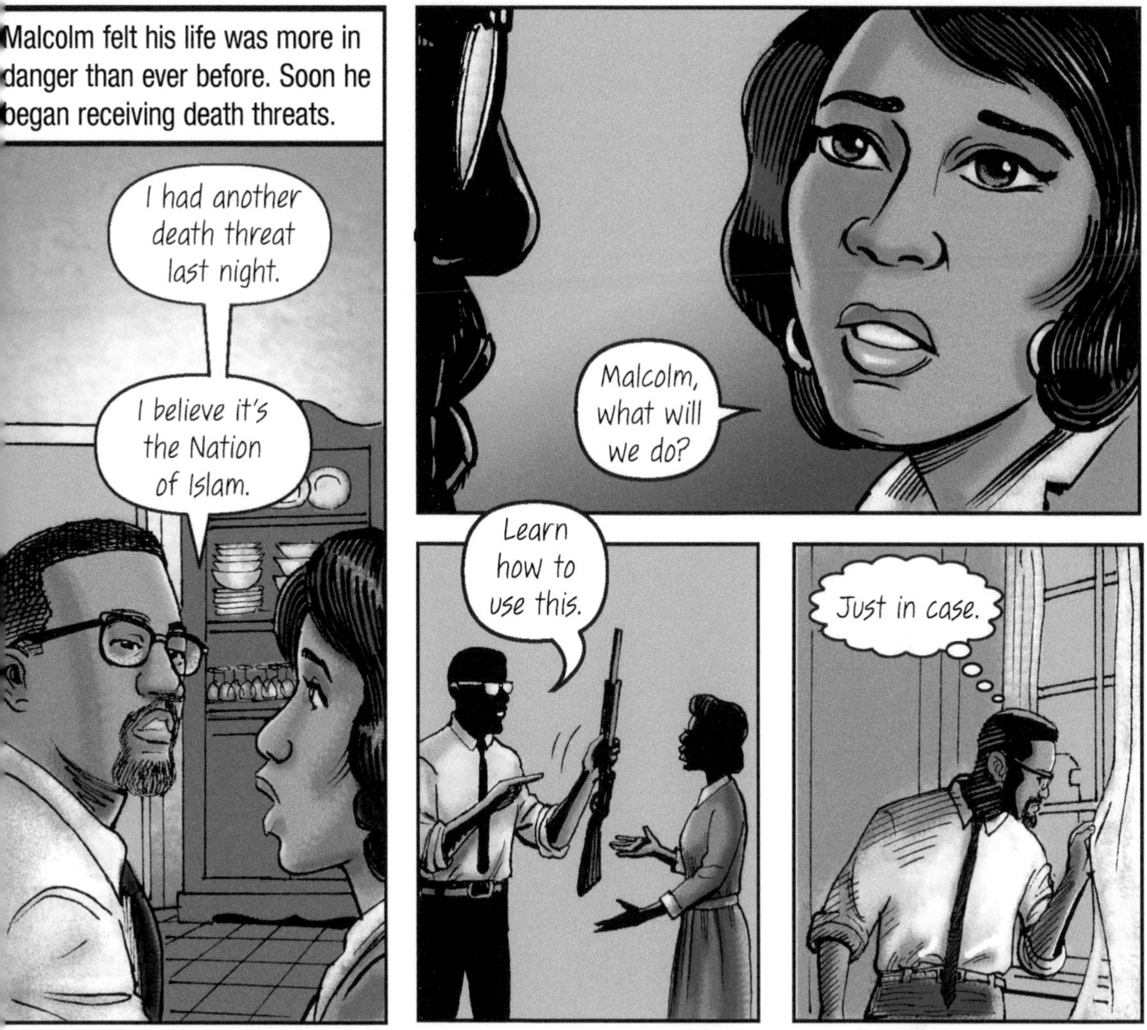
Malcolm felt his life was more in danger than ever before. Soon he began receiving death threats.
I had another death threat last night.
I believe it's the Nation of Islam.
Malcolm, what will we do?
Learn how to use this.
Just in case.

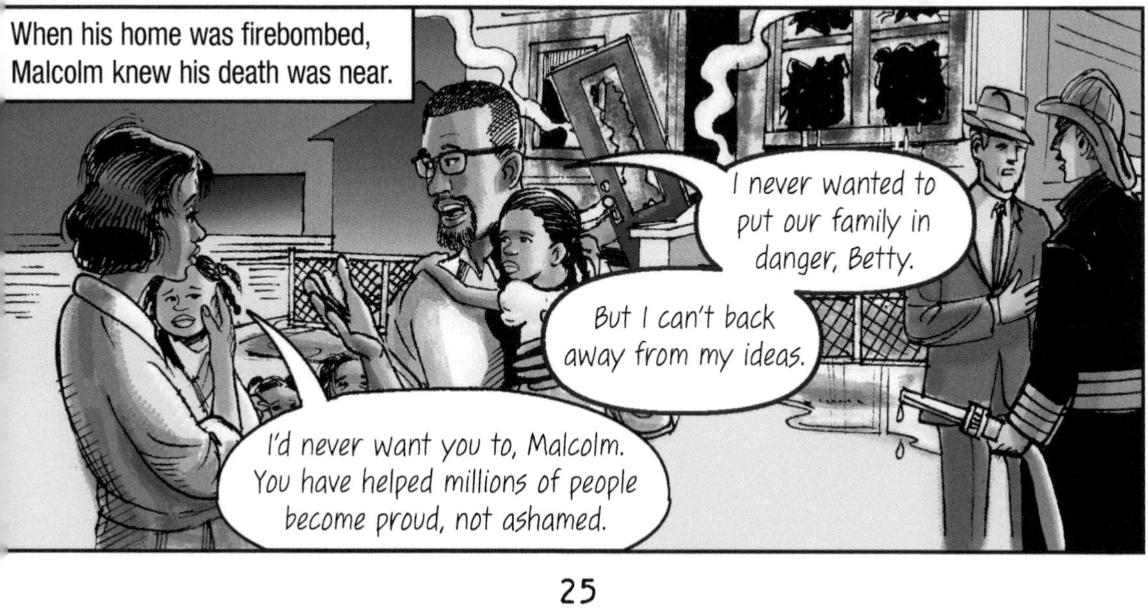
When his home was firebombed, Malcolm knew his death was near.
I never wanted to put our family in danger, Betty.
But I can't back away from my ideas.
I'd never want you to, Malcolm. You have helped millions of people become proud, not ashamed.

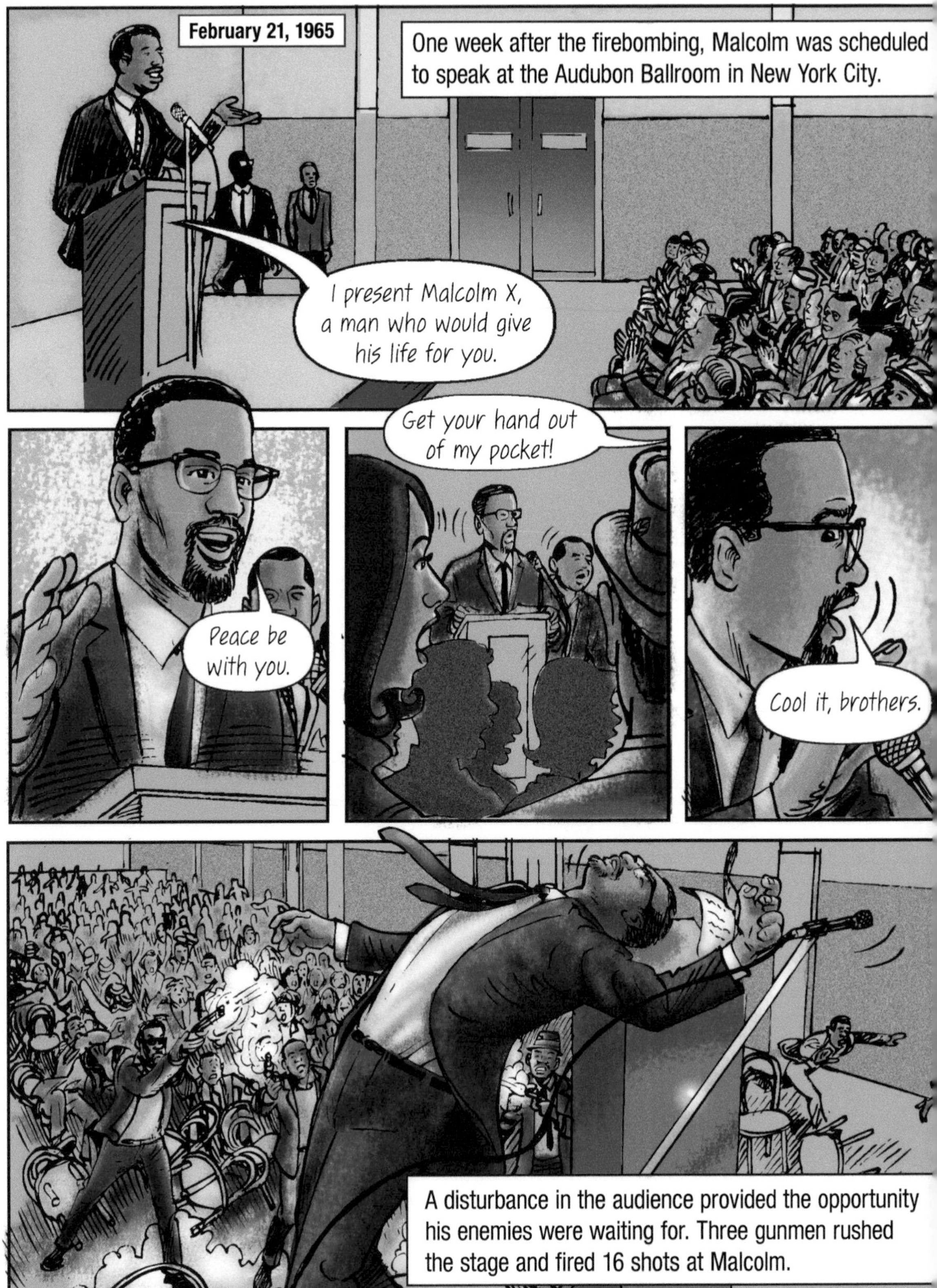

February 21, 1965
One week after the firebombing, Malcolm was scheduled to speak at the Audubon Ballroom in New York City.
I present Malcolm X, a man who would give his life for you.
Peace be with you.
Get your hand out of my pocket!
Cool it, brothers.
A disturbance in the audience provided the opportunity his enemies were waiting for. Three gunmen rushed the stage and fired 16 shots at Malcolm.

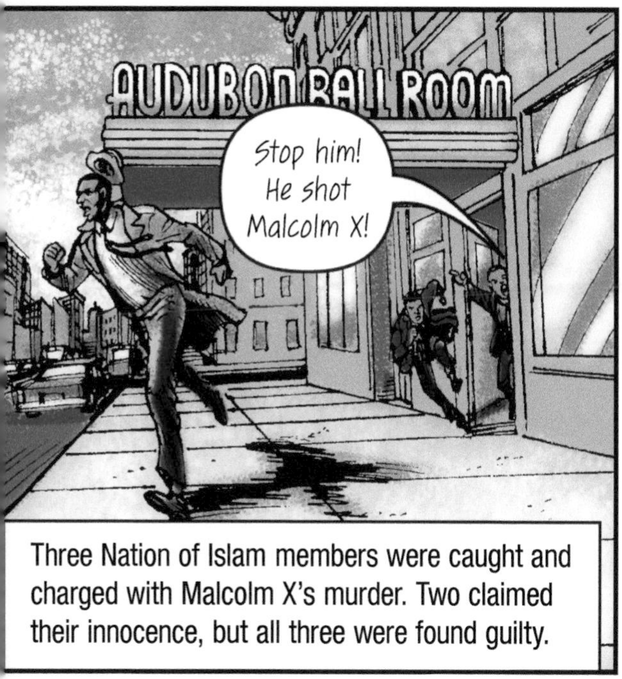

AUDUBON BALLROOM
Stop him! He shot Malcolm X!
Three Nation of Islam members were caught and charged with Malcolm X's murder. Two claimed their innocence, but all three were found guilty.

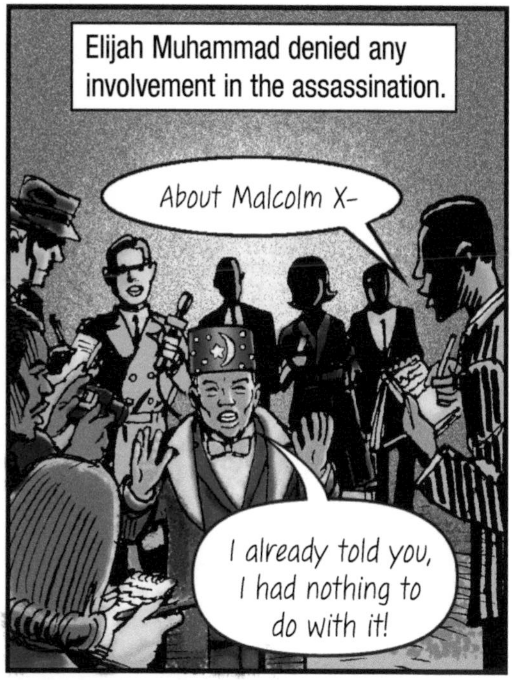

Elijah Muhammad denied any involvement in the assassination.
About Malcolm X-
I already told you, I had nothing to do with it!

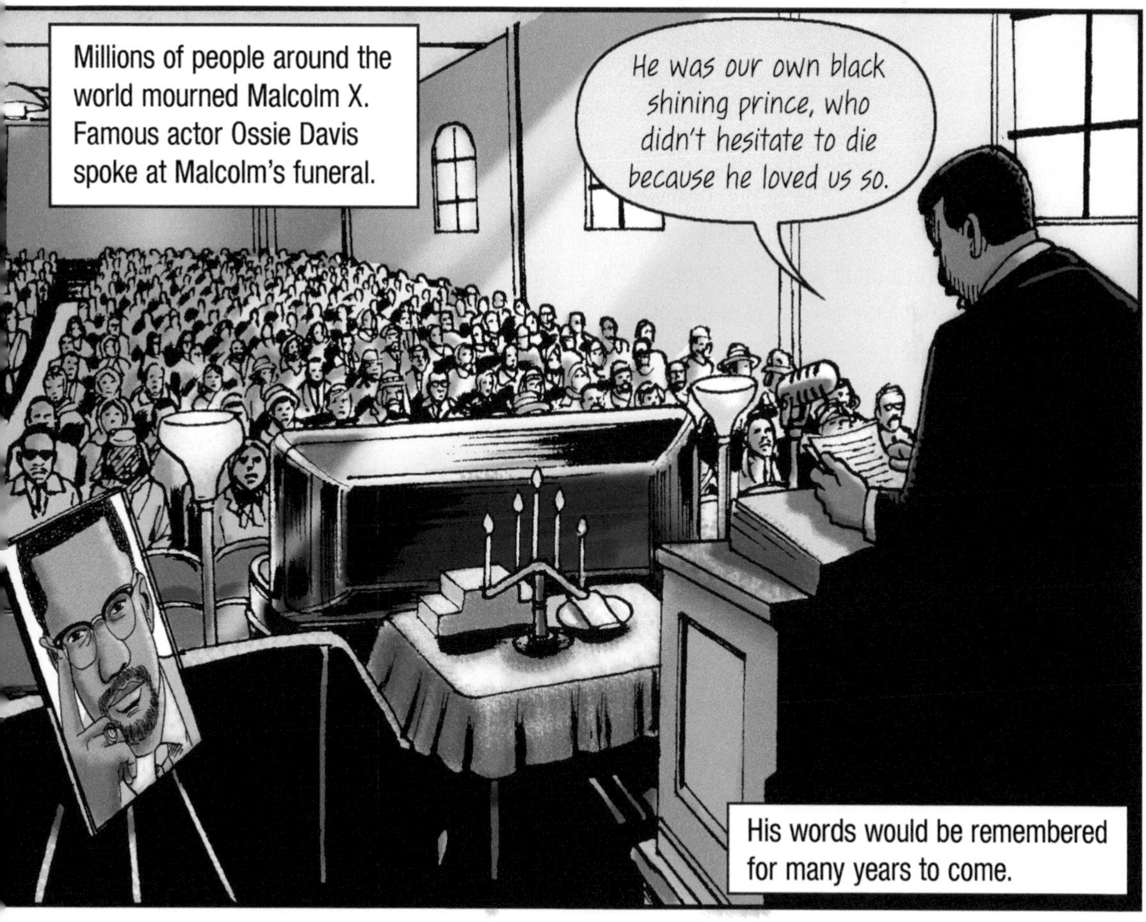

Millions of people around the world mourned Malcolm X. Famous actor Ossie Davis spoke at Malcolm's funeral.
He was our own black shining prince, who didn't hesitate to die because he loved us so.
His words would be remembered for many years to come.

MORE ABOUT MALCOLM X

Although labeled by the public as a militant black man, Malcolm X had a likeable personality and charm. He often wore a smile and liked to make people laugh. He spoke in a way that young and old, educated and uneducated would understand.

Malcolm had a difficult childhood. When he was just six years old, his father was hit by a streetcar and killed. Some people believed he had been beaten and pushed onto the tracks by white racists. When he was 13 years old, Malcolm's mother was sent to a mental hospital. Malcolm and his 10 siblings were sent to separate foster homes. He dropped out of school after the eighth grade and soon became involved in criminal activities.

After prison Malcolm continued to read books on history, religion, and philosophy. He slept only four hours each night. He hoped that the black community would follow his example and become as educated as possible. He said, "Education is the passport to the future, for tomorrow belongs to those who prepare for it today."

Malcolm's wife and other members of his family continued to spread Malcolm's ideas after his death. The civil rights movement continued throughout the 1960s and helped gain equality for African Americans in the workplace and society. The struggle against racism, however, continues to this day.

Malcolm X expressed the struggles and attitudes of the African American in a way that hadn't been voiced before. He died before being able to fully explore his newfound ideas on race, equality, and unity. Nonetheless, Malcolm X played an important role in the struggle for human rights and left behind a lasting legacy.

I BELIEVE IN HUMAN BEINGS,
AND THAT ALL HUMAN BEINGS
SHOULD BE RESPECTED AS SUCH,
REGARDLESS OF THEIR COLOR.

—MALCOLM X

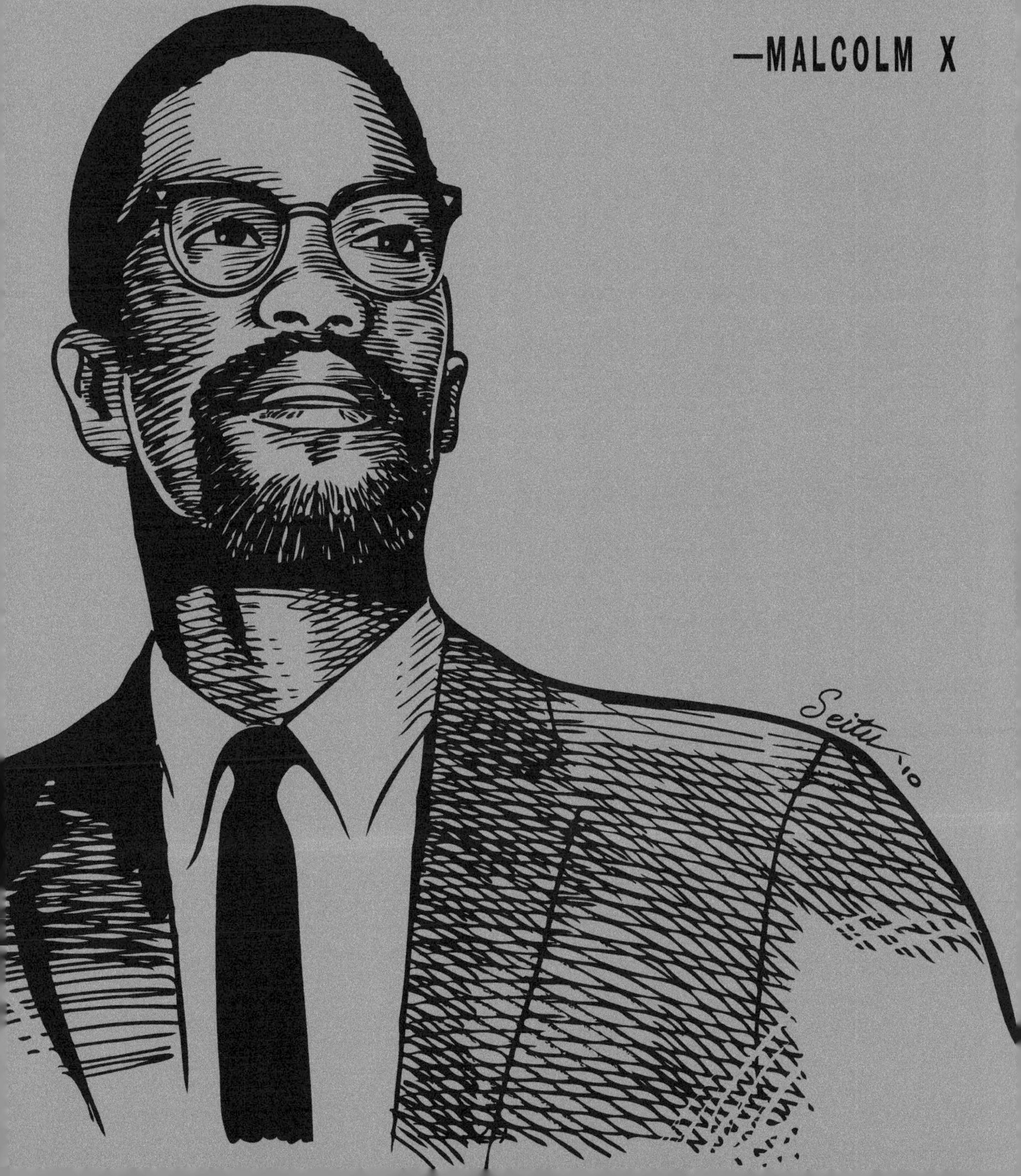
Seitu '10

GLOSSARY

articulate (ar-TIK-yuh-luht)—able to express oneself clearly in words

assassinate (uh-sa-suh-NAYT)—to murder a well-known or important person, such as a president

compromise (KAHM-pruh-myz)—an agreement that people with different views reach after each gives up some demands

equality (i-KWAH-luh-tee)—the same rights for everyone

hostile (HOSS-tuhl)—unfriendly or angry

hypocrite (HIP-uh-krit)—someone who pretends to be loyal, honest, or good

ignorant (IG-nur-uhnt)—not educated, or not knowing about many things

imprison (im-PRIZ-uhn)—to put someone in prison, or to lock the person up

influential (in-floo-EN-shuhl)—having the power to change or affect someone or something

justice (JUHSS-tiss)—fair behavior or treatment

militant (MIL-uh-tuhnt)—prepared to fight or be very aggressive in support of a cause

mourn (MORN)—to be very sad and miss someone who has died

passionate (PASH-uh-nit)—having or showing very strong feelings

pilgrimage (PIL-gruhm-uhj)—a trip to an important religious place

revolution (rev-uh-LOO-shun)—a rebellion by a group of people against a system of government or a way of life

scorn (SKORN)—to treat with a feeling of hatred or disrespect

segregation (seg-ruh-GAY-shuhn)—the practice of keeping groups of people apart, especially based on race

spokesperson (SPOKES-pur-suhn)—someone who is chosen to speak publicly for a group

READ MORE

Banting, Erinn. *The Civil Rights Movement.* African American History. New York: Weigl Publishers, 2009.

Gormley, Beatrice. *Malcolm X: A Revolutionary Voice.* Sterling Biographies. New York: Sterling Publishing, 2008.

Mis, Melody S. *Meet Malcolm X.* Civil Rights Leaders. New York: PowerKids Press, 2008.

INTERNET SITES

FactHound offers a safe, fun way to find Internet sites related to this book. All of the sites on FactHound have been researched by our staff.

Here's all you do: Visit *www.facthound.com*

Type in this code: 9781429654715

Super-cool stuff!

Check out projects, games and lots more at
www.capstonekids.com

INDEX

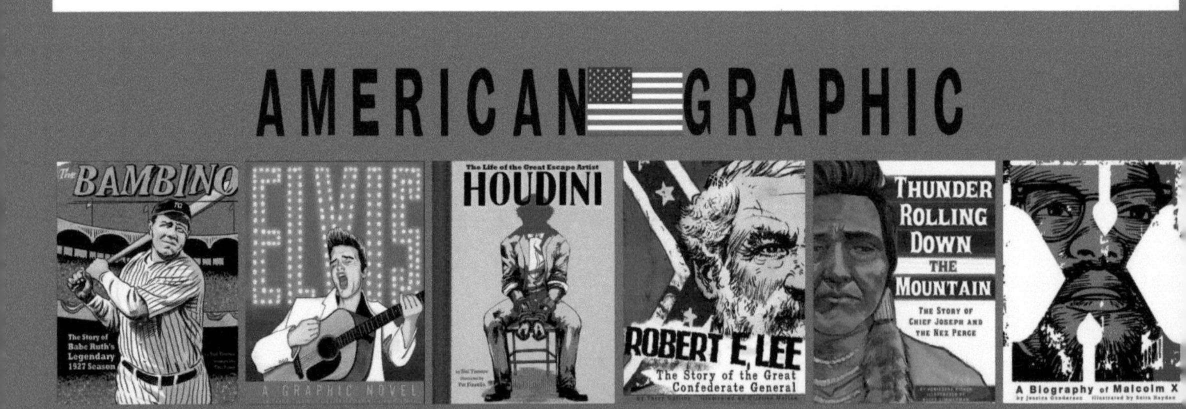
The BAMBINO
The Story of Babe Ruth's Legendary 1927 Season
ELVIS
A GRAPHIC NOVEL
The Life of the Great Escape Artist
HOUDINI
ROBERT E. LEE
The Story of the Great Confederate General
THUNDER ROLLING DOWN THE MOUNTAIN
THE STORY OF CHIEF JOSEPH AND THE NEZ PERCE
A Biography of Malcolm X